Collins
INTERNATIONAL PRIMARY SCIENCE

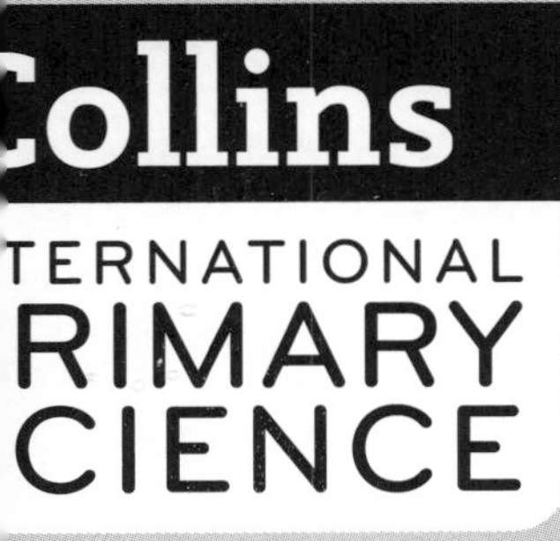

Progress Book 2

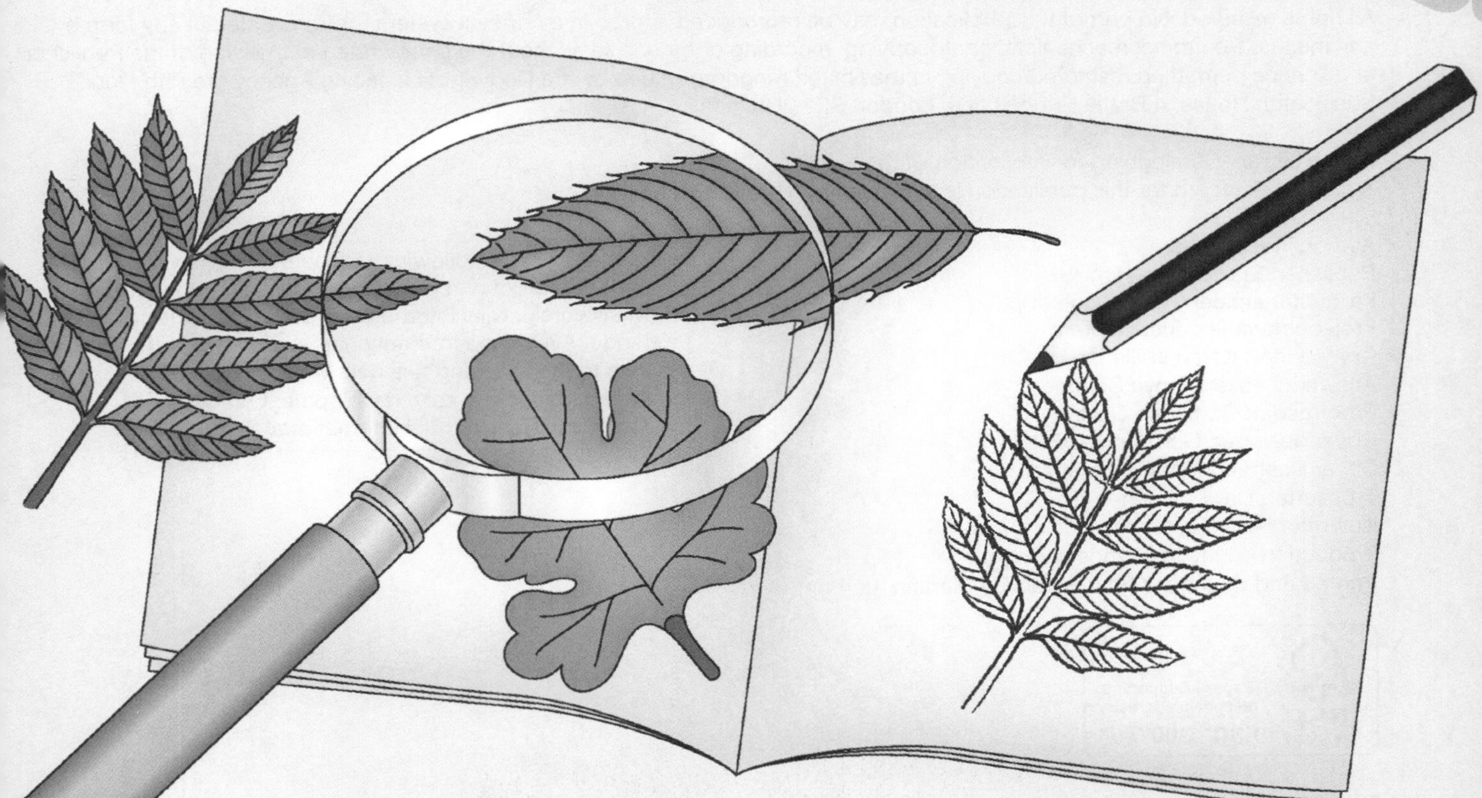

T0382086

Student's Book

William Collins' dream of knowledge for all began with the publication of his first book in 1819.
A self-educated mill worker, he not only enriched millions of lives, but also founded a flourishing publishing house.
Today, staying true to this spirit, Collins books are packed with inspiration, innovation and practical expertise.
They place you at the centre of a world of possibility and give you exactly what you need to explore it.

Collins. Freedom to teach.

Published by Collins

An imprint of HarperCollins*Publishers*
The News Building, 1 London Bridge Street, London, SE1 9GF, UK

HarperCollins*Publishers*
Macken House, 39/40 Mayor Street Upper, Dublin 1, D01 C9W8, Ireland

Browse the complete Collins catalogue at
www.collins.co.uk

© HarperCollins*Publishers* Limited 2023

10 9 8 7 6 5 4 3 2 1

ISBN 978-0-00-865486-3

All rights reserved. No part of this publication may be reproduced, stored in a retrieval system, or transmitted in any form by any means, electronic, mechanical, photocopying, recording or otherwise, without the prior written permission of the Publisher or a licence permitting restricted copying in the United Kingdom issued by the Copyright Licensing Agency Ltd, 5th Floor, Shackleton House, 4 Battle Bridge Lane, London SE1 2HX.

British Library Cataloguing-in-Publication Data
A catalogue record for this publication is available from the British Library.

Author: Tracy Wiles
Publisher: Elaine Higgleton
Product manager: Holly Woolnough
Project manager: Just Content
Copy editor: Karen Williams
Answer checker: Tanya Solomons
Proofreader: Catherine Dakin
Cover designer: Gordon MacGilp
Cover illustration: Ann Paganuzzi
Typesetter: David Jimenez
Illustrator: Ann Paganuzzi
Production controller: Lyndsey Rogers
Printed and bound in Great Britain by Martins the Printers

With thanks to the following teachers for reviewing materials in proof and providing valuable feedback: Sylvie Meurein, Nilai International School; Gabriel Kehinde, Avi-Cenna International School; and with thanks to the following teachers who provided feedback during the early development stage: Najihah binti Roslan, Nilai International School.

FSC™ MIX
Paper | Supporting responsible forestry
FSC™ C007454
www.fsc.org

This book is produced from independently certified FSC™ paper to ensure responsible forest management.
For more information visit: harpercollins.co.uk/green

The publishers gratefully acknowledge the permission granted to reproduce the copyright material in this book. Every effort has been made to trace copyright holders and to obtain their permission for the use of copyright material. The publishers will gladly receive any information enabling them to rectify any error or omission at the first opportunity.

Cambridge International copyright material in this publication is reproduced under licence and remains the intellectual property of Cambridge Assessment International Education

This text has not been through the Cambridge International endorsement process.

Contents

Topic 3 Matter and materials

Topic 4 Forces

Topic 5 Light and electricity

Topic 6 The Earth's crust

How to use this book

This book is full of questions. Each set of questions can be completed at the end of each unit.

The questions allow you to practise the things you've learned. They will help you understand topics that you might need more practice of. They will also show you the topics that you are most confident with. Your teacher can use your answers to give you feedback and support.

At the end of each test, there is a space to put the date that you completed it. There is also a blank box. Your teacher might use it to:

- sign, when they have marked your answers
- write a short comment on your work.

Date: ____________________

Now look at and think about each of the *I can* statements.

Pages 7 to 15 include a list of *I can* statements. Once you have finished each set of questions, turn to the *I can* statements. Think about each statement: how easy or hard did you find the topic? For each statement, colour in the face that is closest to how you feel:

☺ I can do this ☹ I'm getting there ☹ I need some help.

There are three longer Summative Assessments in the book. These can be completed after each block of topics.

I can statements

At the end of each unit, think about each of the *I can* statements and how easy or hard you find the topic. For each statement, colour in the face that is closest to how you feel.

TOPIC 1 Living things in their environment	
1.1 – Asking questions	**Date:**
I know that scientists learn more about the world by asking and answering questions.	☺ 😐 ☹
I know that scientists measure, observe and read to find answers to their questions.	☺ 😐 ☹
1.2 – What is an environment?	**Date:**
I know that a natural environment has not been changed by people.	☺ 😐 ☹
I know that an environment needs to have everything that plants and animals need to live there.	☺ 😐 ☹
I know that the environment where a plant and animal live is called a habitat.	☺ 😐 ☹
1.3 – Compare natural environments	**Date:**
I can identify the similarities and differences between local environments.	☺ 😐 ☹
I know that environments can be cold, warm, hot, wet or dry.	☺ 😐 ☹
I know that the conditions found in an environment affect which plants and animals can live there.	☺ 😐 ☹
1.4 – Plants in different habitats	**Date:**
I know that the conditions in an environment affect the types of plants found there.	☺ 😐 ☹
I know that different plants are found in different habitats.	☺ 😐 ☹

1.5 – Animals in different habitats	Date:
I know that different animals are found in different habitats.	☺ 😐 ☹
I know that animals live in habitats that provide food, water and shelter.	☺ 😐 ☹
1.6 – Exploring local environments	**Date:**
I know that local environments can have different habitats in them.	☺ 😐 ☹
I can find information about a habitat by investigating it.	☺ 😐 ☹
I can use a block graph to share what I find out.	☺ 😐 ☹
1.7 – Investigate a local environment	**Date:**
I can find information about a habitat by investigating it.	☺ 😐 ☹
I know that an investigation involves recording my observations and sharing my findings.	☺ 😐 ☹
TOPIC 2 Humans and other animals	
2.1 – Humans and other animals	**Date:**
I know that all animals have a head, body and limbs.	☺ 😐 ☹
I know that many animals have a nose and ears.	☺ 😐 ☹
I know that the body parts of different animals look different.	☺ 😐 ☹
I know that all animals have a skin covering, although they are different for different animals.	☺ 😐 ☹
2.2 – Animals and their offspring	**Date:**
I know all animals have offspring.	☺ 😐 ☹

I know that offspring grow and change as they get older.	☺ 😐 ☹
I know that some young animals need an adult animal to look after them.	☺ 😐 ☹
2.3 – Do we look like our parents?	**Date:**
I know that offspring are born with a combination of features from their parents.	☺ 😐 ☹
I know that we inherit our features from our parents, which is why the offspring of humans and other animals look similar to their parents.	☺ 😐 ☹
2.4 – Keeping healthy	**Date:**
I know that humans need food to stay healthy.	☺ 😐 ☹
I know that we need to keep our bodies clean to stay healthy.	☺ 😐 ☹
2.5 – Diet and exercise are important	**Date:**
I know I need to eat healthy food to stay fit and well.	☺ 😐 ☹
I know my body needs exercise every day to stay healthy.	☺ 😐 ☹
I know that exercise makes our bodies stronger and more flexible.	☺ 😐 ☹
2.6 – Signs of illness	**Date:**
I know that germs entering our body can make us sick.	☺ 😐 ☹
I know that a fever, sore throat, coughing or sneezing are all different signs that show I am sick.	☺ 😐 ☹
I know that germs can spread from one person to another.	☺ 😐 ☹

2.7 – Human teeth	Date:
I know that humans start getting permanent teeth when they are about 6 years old.	☺ 😐 ☹
I know that humans have different kinds of teeth that do different things to break food into smaller pieces.	☺ 😐 ☹
I know I need to brush my teeth every morning and night to look after them.	☺ 😐 ☹
2.8 – Dentists and science	**Date:**
I know that a doctor who takes care of our teeth and gums is called a dentist.	☺ 😐 ☹
I know that science helps dentists to do their jobs.	☺ 😐 ☹
TOPIC 3 Matter and materials	
3.1 – Measuring	**Date:**
I can measure to find out how much there is of something.	☺ 😐 ☹
I can use different objects to measure with.	☺ 😐 ☹
I know that if I want to compare objects, I need to measure them using the same thing.	☺ 😐 ☹
3.2 – Natural materials	**Date:**
I know that some materials occur naturally in the environment.	☺ 😐 ☹
I can identify stone, wood, cotton, leather, wool, horn and feathers as natural materials.	☺ 😐 ☹
3.3 – Manufactured materials	**Date:**
I know that some items are manufactured using natural materials.	☺ 😐 ☹
I can identify concrete, plastics, glass, metals, paper and rubber as manufactured materials.	☺ 😐 ☹

3.4 – Properties of materials	Date:
I know that different materials have different properties.	☺ 😐 ☹
I know that materials can have more than one property.	☺ 😐 ☹
3.5 – Hard or soft?	**Date:**
I can group materials according to their properties.	☺ 😐 ☹
I know that hardness and softness are properties of materials.	☺ 😐 ☹
I can identify materials that are harder than others.	☺ 😐 ☹
I can identify surfaces that are harder than others.	☺ 😐 ☹
3.6 – Strength	**Date:**
I know that strong materials do not break easily.	☺ 😐 ☹
I know that strength is not the same as hardness.	☺ 😐 ☹
3.7 – Flexibility	**Date:**
I know that flexible materials can bend, stretch or be squashed.	☺ 😐 ☹
I know that rigid materials cannot bend or change shape.	☺ 😐 ☹
3.8 – Uses of materials	**Date:**
I know that materials are chosen for purposes, based on their properties.	☺ 😐 ☹
3.9 – Changing materials	**Date:**
I know that some changes can turn a material into a different material.	☺ 😐 ☹

3.10 – Sports equipment	Date:
I know that sports equipment has changed over time.	☺ 😐 ☹
I know that science has been used to make sports equipment better.	☺ 😐 ☹
TOPIC 4 Forces	
4.1 – Modelling	**Date:**
I know that a model shows what something looks like or how it works.	☺ 😐 ☹
I know that pushes and pulls are forces that make objects move.	☺ 😐 ☹
4.2 – Forces and movement	**Date:**
I know that a push or a pull force can make an object start moving.	☺ 😐 ☹
I know that a push force acting in the opposite direction to a moving object stops it.	☺ 😐 ☹
4.3 – Changing the shape of an object	**Date:**
I know that forces can change the shape of things.	☺ 😐 ☹
I know that forces can cause damage or help make objects.	☺ 😐 ☹
4.4 – Speeding up and slowing down	**Date:**
I know that a force can make an object speed up or slow down.	☺ 😐 ☹
I know that a force can make an object start to move.	☺ 😐 ☹
I know that a force can stop an object from moving.	☺ 😐 ☹
4.5 – Changing direction	**Date:**
I can use a force to make an object change direction.	☺ 😐 ☹

TOPIC 5 Light and electricity	
5.1 – Sources of light	**Date:**
I know that things that give out light are called sources of light.	☺ 😐 ☹
I know that the Sun is a natural source of light.	☺ 😐 ☹
I can identify human-made sources of light, such as candles, torches, lamps and car headlights.	☺ 😐 ☹
5.2 – Light and dark	**Date:**
I know that we need light to see.	☺ 😐 ☹
I know that it is dark when there is no light.	☺ 😐 ☹
5.3 – Lighting in our homes	**Date:**
I know that people have been lighting their homes for a long time.	☺ 😐 ☹
I know that what we use to light our homes has changed over time.	☺ 😐 ☹
I know that people use electricity to light their homes today.	☺ 😐 ☹
5.4 – Where is the Sun?	**Date:**
I can describe the apparent movement of the Sun during the daytime.	☺ 😐 ☹
5.5 – Using electricity	**Date:**
I know that electricity is helpful and also dangerous.	☺ 😐 ☹
I can identify what we use electricity for every day.	☺ 😐 ☹
I know how to use electricity safely so I do not get hurt.	☺ 😐 ☹

5.6 – What is a circuit?	**Date:**
I know that a circuit is a path that electricity follows.	☺ 😐 ☹
I know that cells, wires and lamps can be used to build a simple circuit.	☺ 😐 ☹
5.7 – Building circuits	**Date:**
I know that electricity can only move through a complete, or closed circuit.	☺ 😐 ☹
I know that the components need to be joined properly to make a closed circuit.	☺ 😐 ☹
I know that when a circuit is closed, a lamp will light up.	☺ 😐 ☹
TOPIC 6 The Earth's crust	
6.1 – Using sources	**Date:**
I know that the Earth's crust has materials that are useful to people.	☺ 😐 ☹
I know that mines change the natural environment forever.	☺ 😐 ☹
6.2 – Different types of rock	**Date:**
I know that there are many different types of rocks.	☺ 😐 ☹
I can identify sandstone, limestone, marble, granite and slate as different types of rocks.	☺ 😐 ☹
6.3 – Rocks are useful	**Date:**
I know that different types of rocks are used in different ways.	☺ 😐 ☹
I know that the uses of rock depend on its properties.	☺ 😐 ☹
6.4 – Mining the Earth	**Date:**
I know that mines are places where people dig out stone and minerals from the Earth.	☺ 😐 ☹
I know that mining changes the natural environment.	☺ 😐 ☹

6.5 – Mining in Madagascar	Date:
I know that mining provides jobs for people.	☺ 😐 ☹
I know that mining can damage the natural environment.	☺ 😐 ☹
I know that science can help us to find ways to repair the environment and care for it.	☺ 😐 ☹

1 Look at the pictures. How are the scientists trying to find answers to their questions?

What question could each scientist be asking?

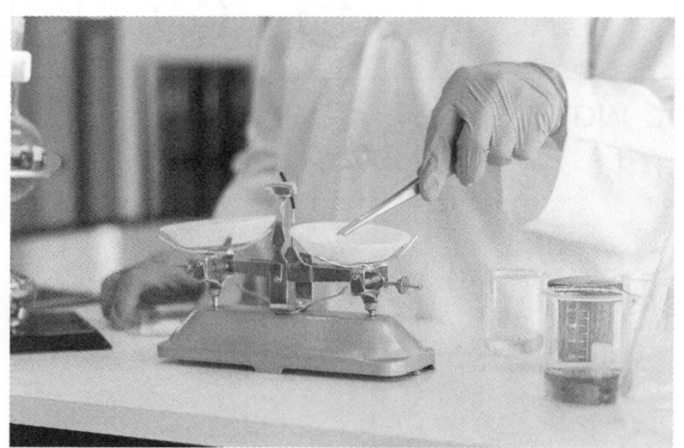

a ______________________

Question: ______________________

____

____

____

b ______________________

Question: ______________________

____

____

____

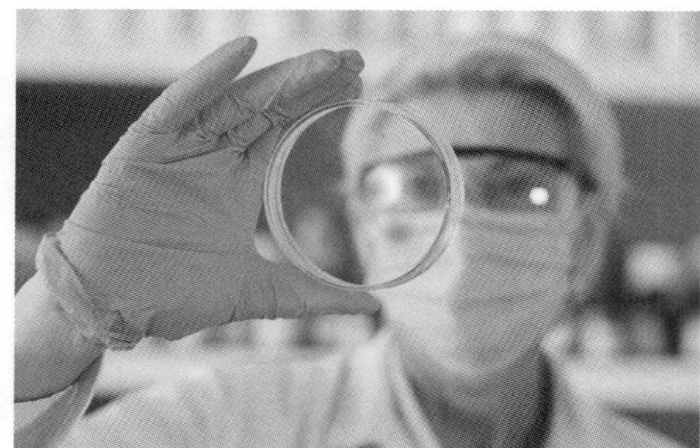

c ______________________

Question: ______________________

____

____

____

d ______________________

Question: ______________________

____

____

____

2 Look at the picture. What questions could you ask to find out more about what you see?

- ____________________
- ____________________
- ____________________
- ____________________
- ____________________

Date: ____________________

Now look at and think about each of the *I can* statements.

1 Draw lines to match each picture to a type of natural environment. Then match each picture to a description.

Natural environment		Description
grassland		flat, grassy
forest		hot, dry, very few plants or animals
desert		wet, salty
mountains		sticky, hot, wet, lots of plants
ocean		rocky, high, cold, windy

2 Look at the picture. Identify the type of environment.

____

____

____

3 Look at the picture below. Name three animals found in their natural habitat.

____

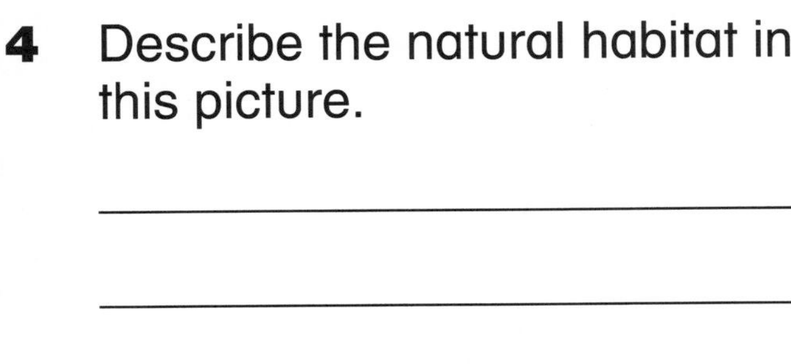

4 Describe the natural habitat in this picture.

____

____

____

____

5 How are the environments in questions 2 and 3 different?

____

____

6 How are the environments in questions 2 and 3 similar?

____

____

Date: _______________________

Now look at and think about each of the *I can* statements.

1 Draw lines to match the plants to their habitats.

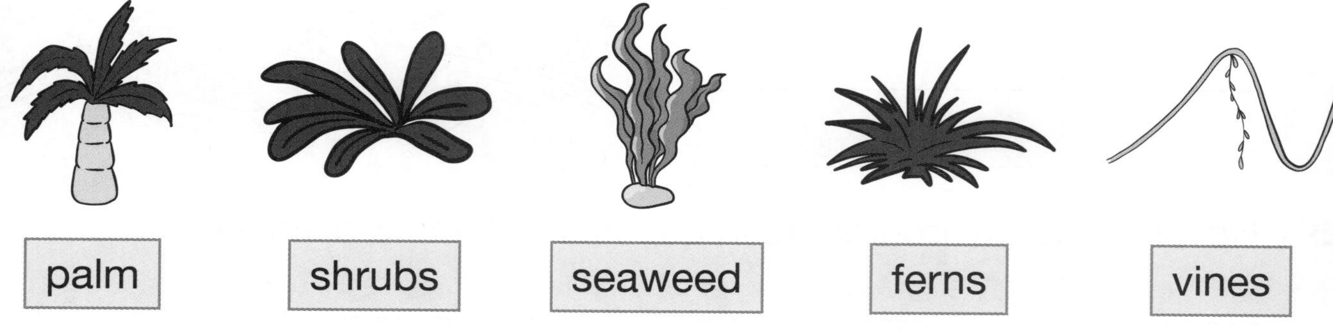

2 Circle the correct words or phrases to complete the sentences.

a Seaweed only grows in **soil / ocean water**.

b Trees need **warm and wet / hot and dry** weather to grow.

c A fern is better suited for the **ocean / rainforest**.

d Coral is better suited for the **ocean / rainforest**.

3 Draw lines to match the animals to their habitats.

desert

polar region

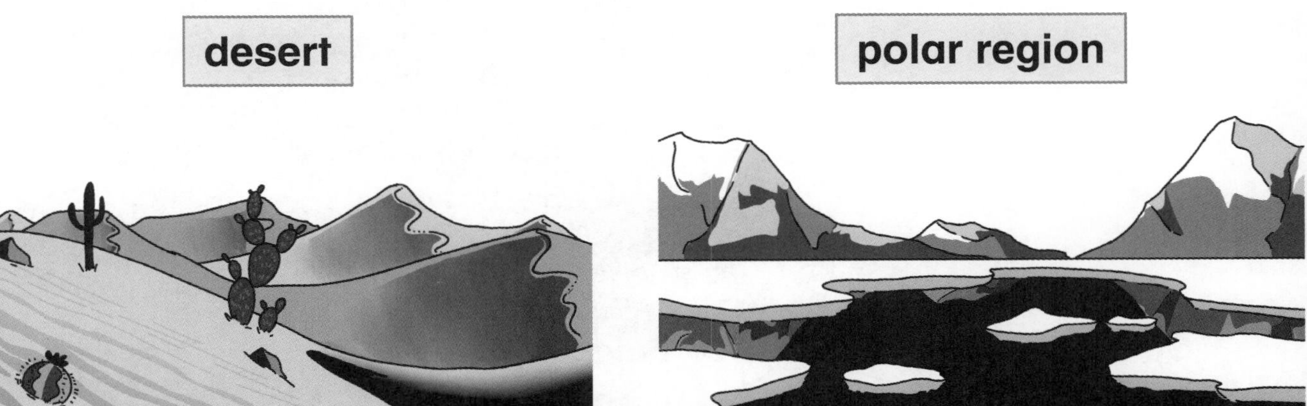

roadrunner

sidewinder snake

polar bear

Arctic fox

puffin

lizard

4 Circle the correct words or phrases to complete the sentences.

a A desert is **hot and dry** / **hot and wet**.

b A polar region is **cold and dry** / **cold with snow**.

c A camel is better suited for the **desert** / **polar region**.

d A snow owl is better suited for the **desert** / **polar region**.

Date: ______________________

Now look at and think about each of the *I can* statements.

Look at the picture.

1 What can you see in this habitat?

____

____

2 What types of plants grow in a habitat like this?

____

3 How many different animals can you see in the picture? Complete the chart.

Type of small animal	How many?
spider	
butterfly	
fly	
ant	
caterpillar	
earthworm	

Type of small animal	How many?
centipede	
snail	
wasp	
beetle	
woodlouse	

4 Colour the block graph to show how many animals of each type you found in the picture in question 1. Use a different colour for each column.

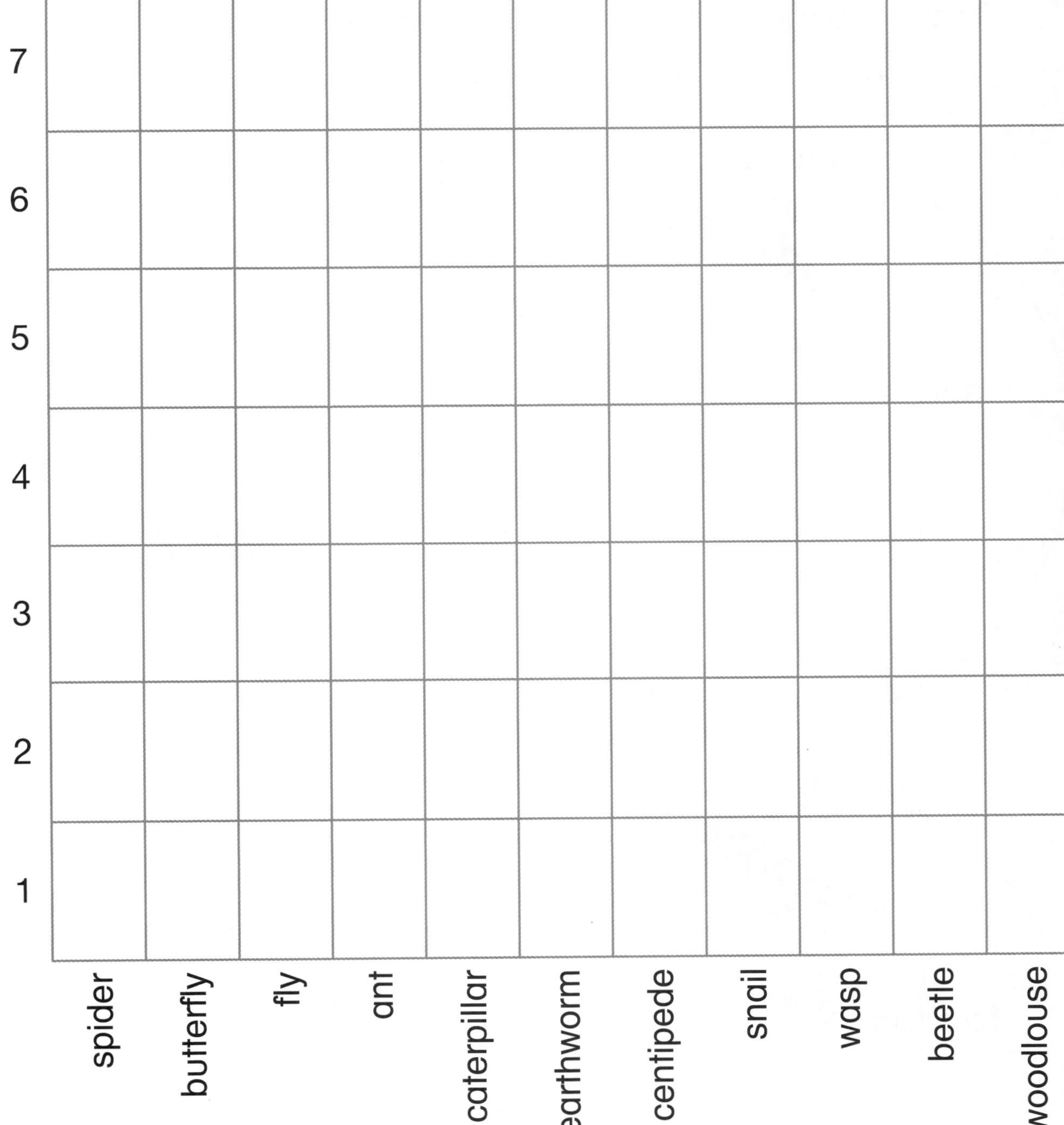

Now look at and think about each of the *I can* statements.

Date: ____________________

1 Use the words in the box to describe each picture. Which words go in more than one circle? One example has already been done for you.

head	body	arms	legs	wings	fins
hair	feathers	scales	shell		

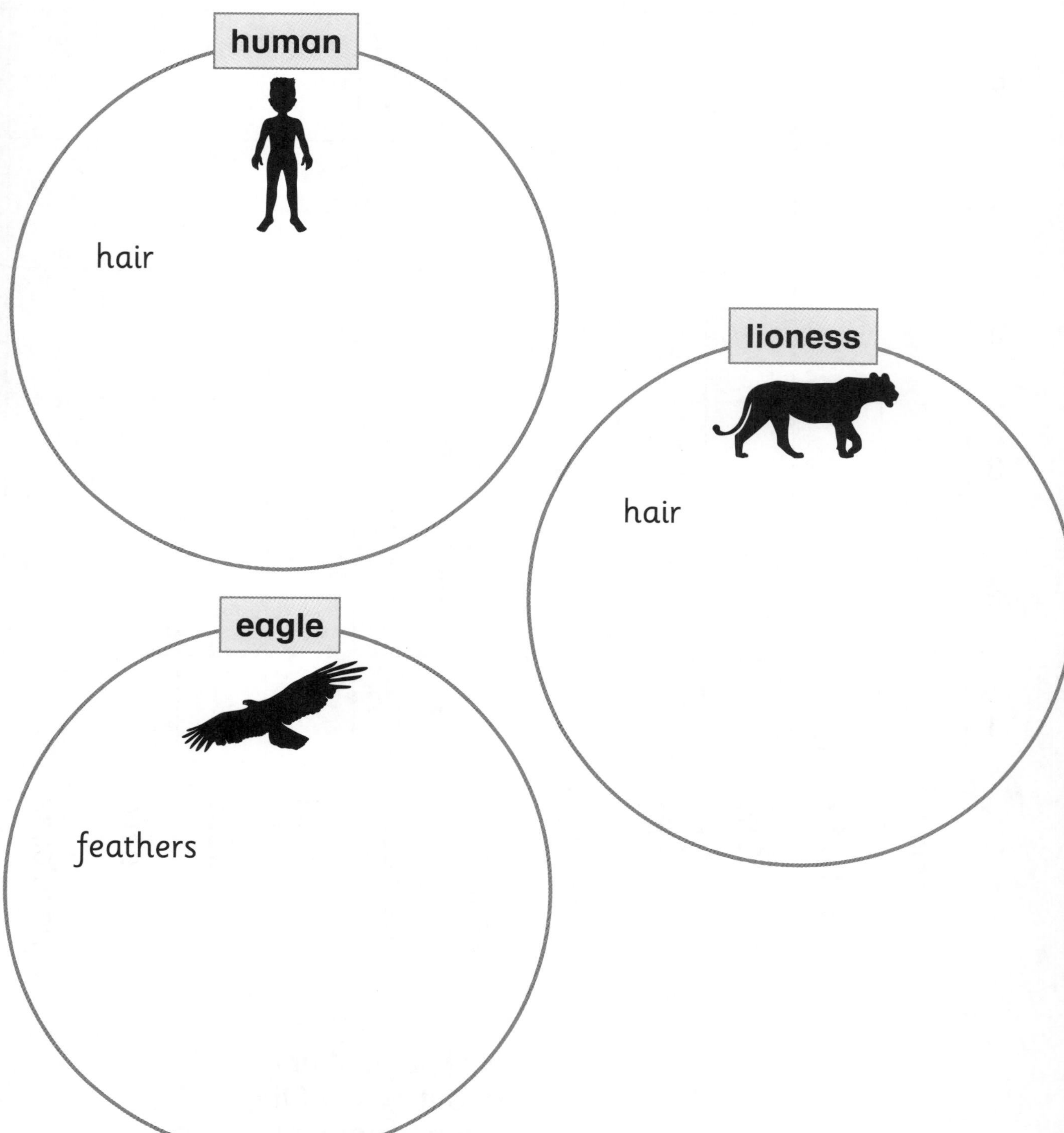

2 Write words in the circles to describe the animal in each picture. Use words from the box. Which words go in more than one circle? One example has already been done for you.

head body arms legs wings fins
hair feathers scales shell

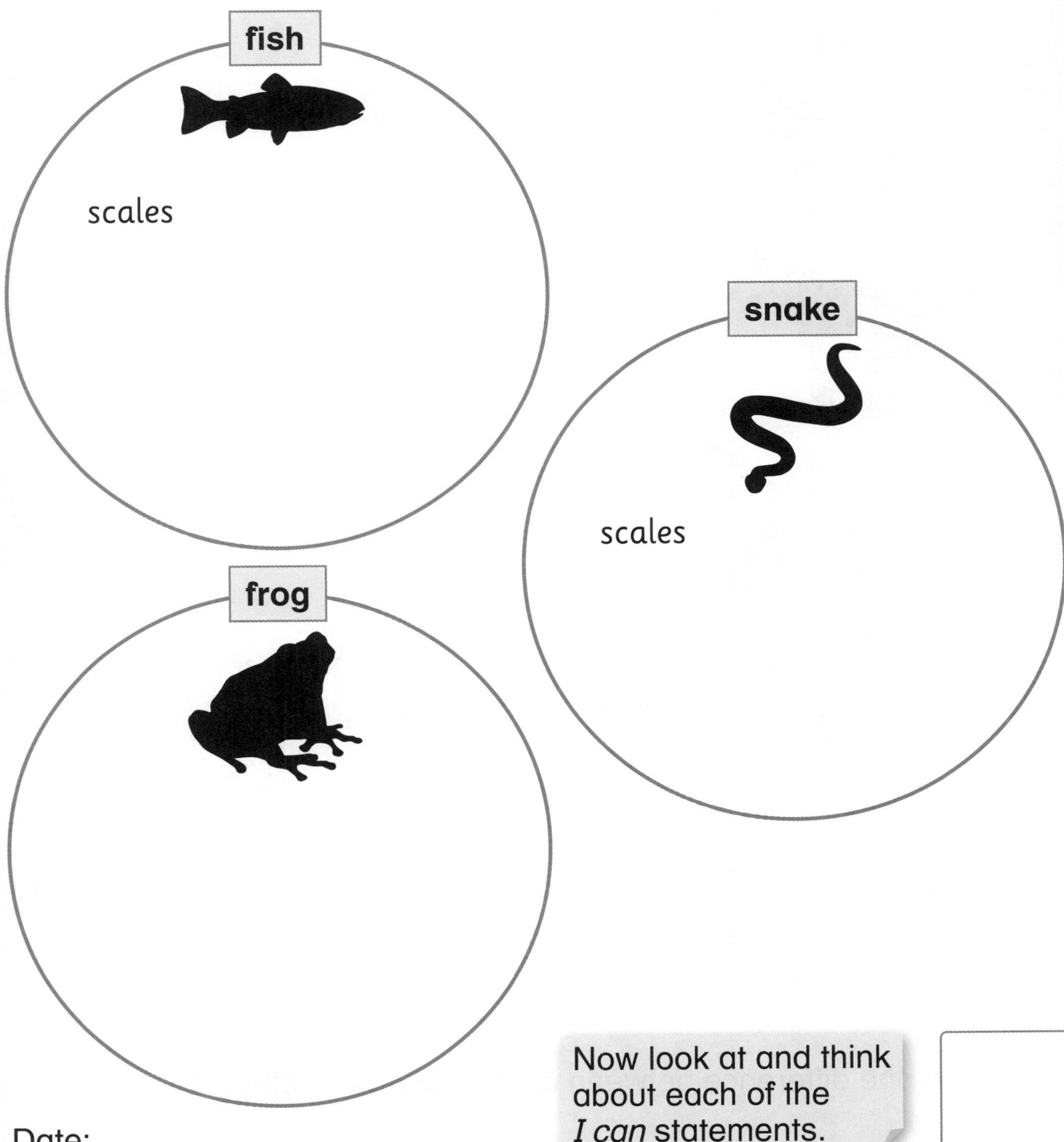

Date: ____________________

Now look at and think about each of the *I can* statements.

1 Draw lines to match each offspring to its animal family.

2 Name one difference between an animal and its offspring.

____

3 Look at the picture.

a Which features does the kitten share with both parents?

____

____

b Which feature is shared with only one parent?

____

4 Look at the picture.

a How is the fawn like its parents?

____

____

b How is the fawn different to its parents?

____

____

Date: ____________________

Now look at and think about each of the *I can* statements.

1 Colour in the healthy foods. Circle the foods you should eat less of.

2 Draw lines from the food to the correct shelves.

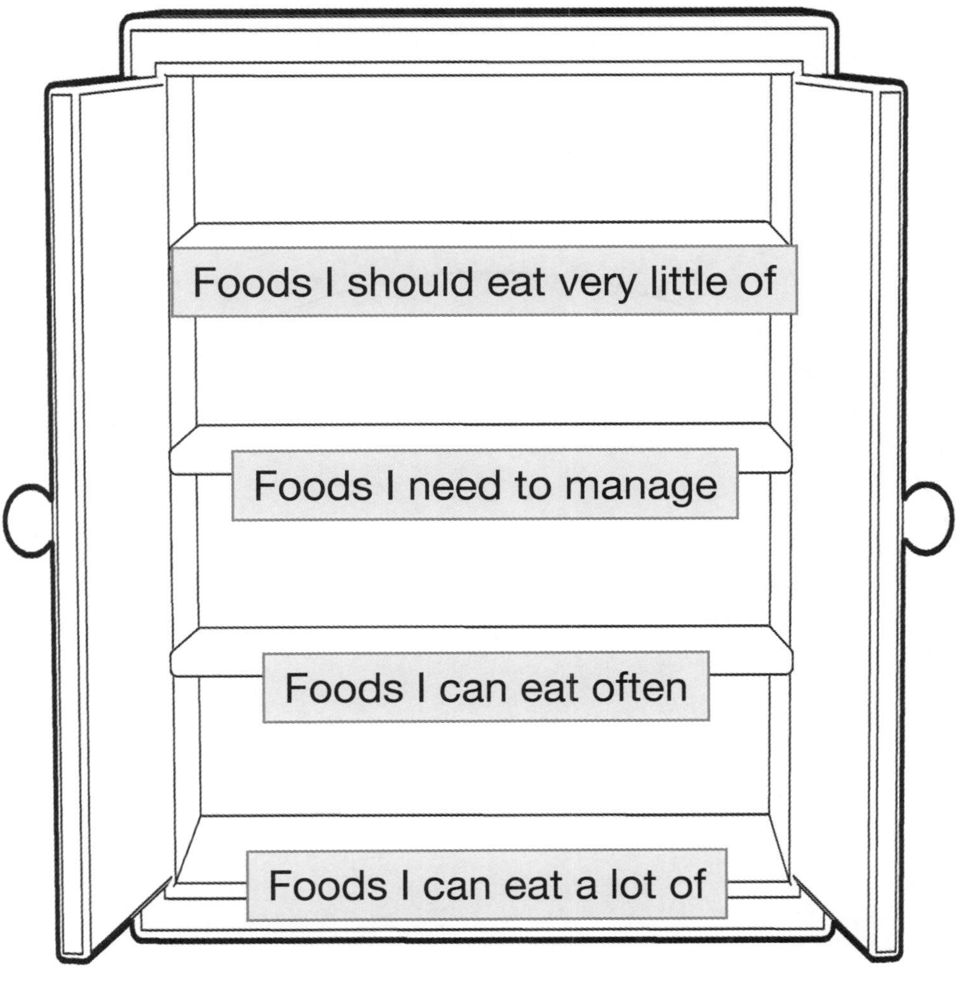

Now look at and think about each of the *I can* statements.

Date: ______________________

1 Draw a healthy meal on the plate. Label each food item you draw.

2 Tick (✓) the pictures that show good exercises to keep you healthy.

3 Draw a picture of something you do to keep fit.

4 Draw a picture of something you do that does not keep you fit.

Now look at and think about each of the *I can* statements.

Date: ____________________

1 What is wrong with the children? Use the words in the box.

fever	very tired	headache	cough
sore stomach	blocked nose	sore throat	

a

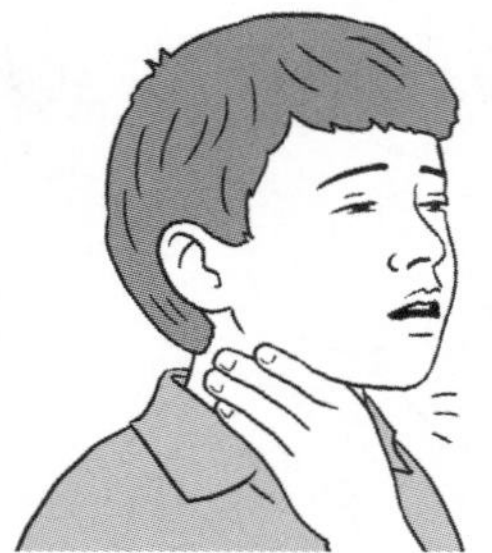

b

c

______________ ______________ ______________

d

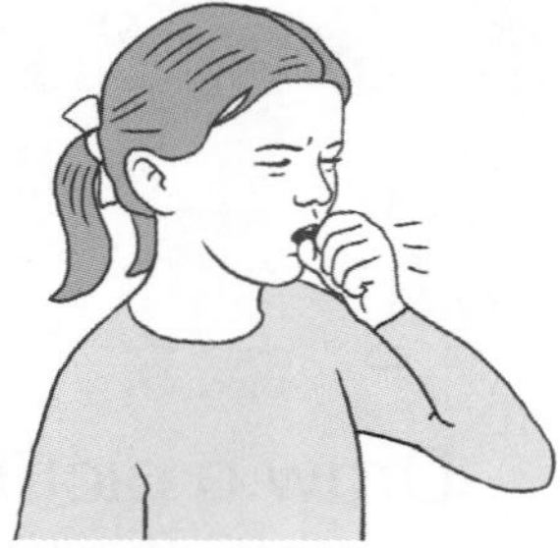

e

______________ ______________

f

g

______________ ______________

2 Answer the questions. Circle the correct answer.

a Do germs make people sick? **Yes** / **No**

b Can you see germs? **Yes** / **No**

3 Look at the picture of the man sneezing.

a What is the man doing wrong?

____

b What should the man do so that he does not spread germs?

____

____

4 Look at the picture of the man coughing.

a What is the man doing wrong?

____

b What should the man do so that he does not spread germs?

____

____

Date: ______________________

Now look at and think about each of the *I can* statements.

1 Label the teeth in the diagram.

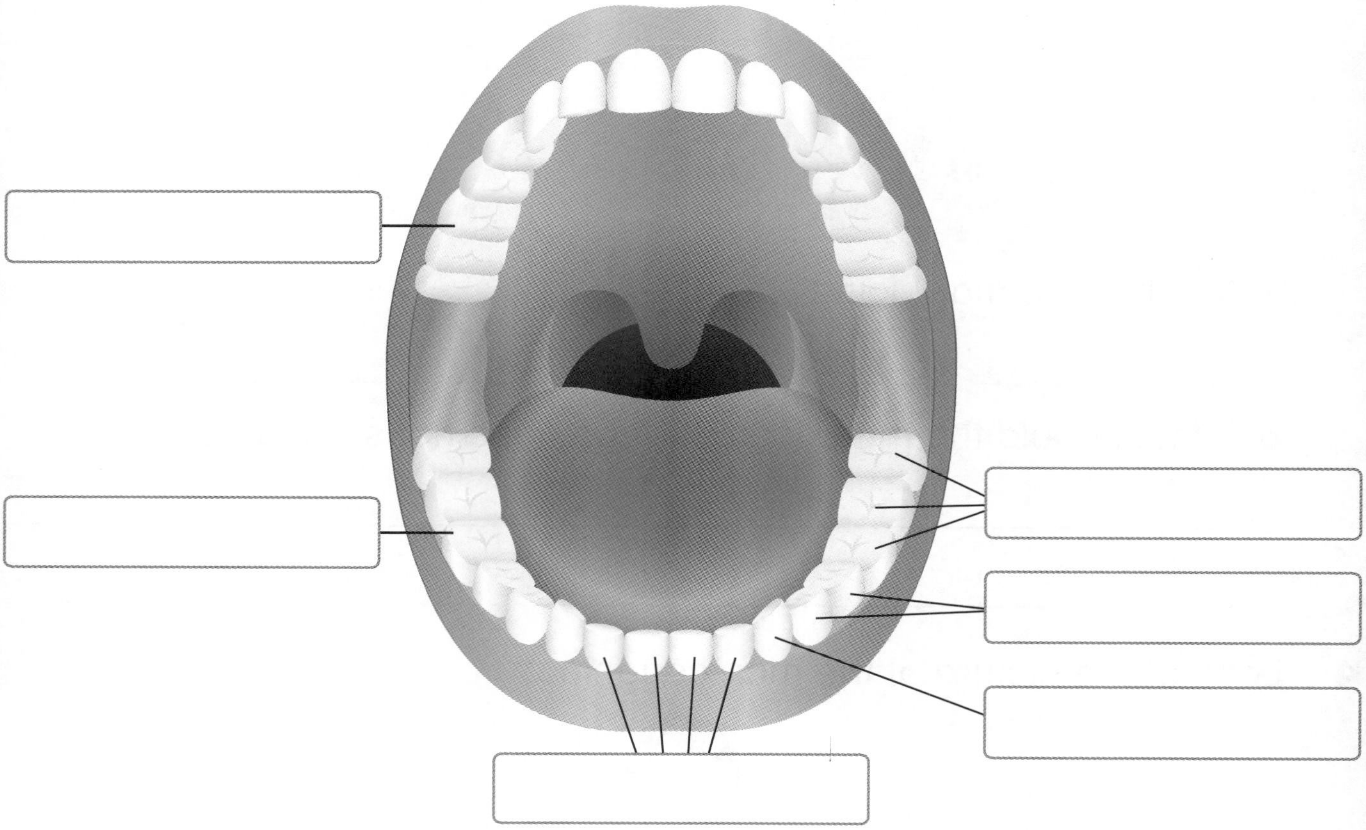

2 Explain what each type of tooth does to your food.

incisor: ____________________

canine: ____________________

premolar: ____________________

molar: ____________________

3 How many permanent teeth does an adult human have?

____

4 Circle the tools that a dentist uses to look after your teeth.

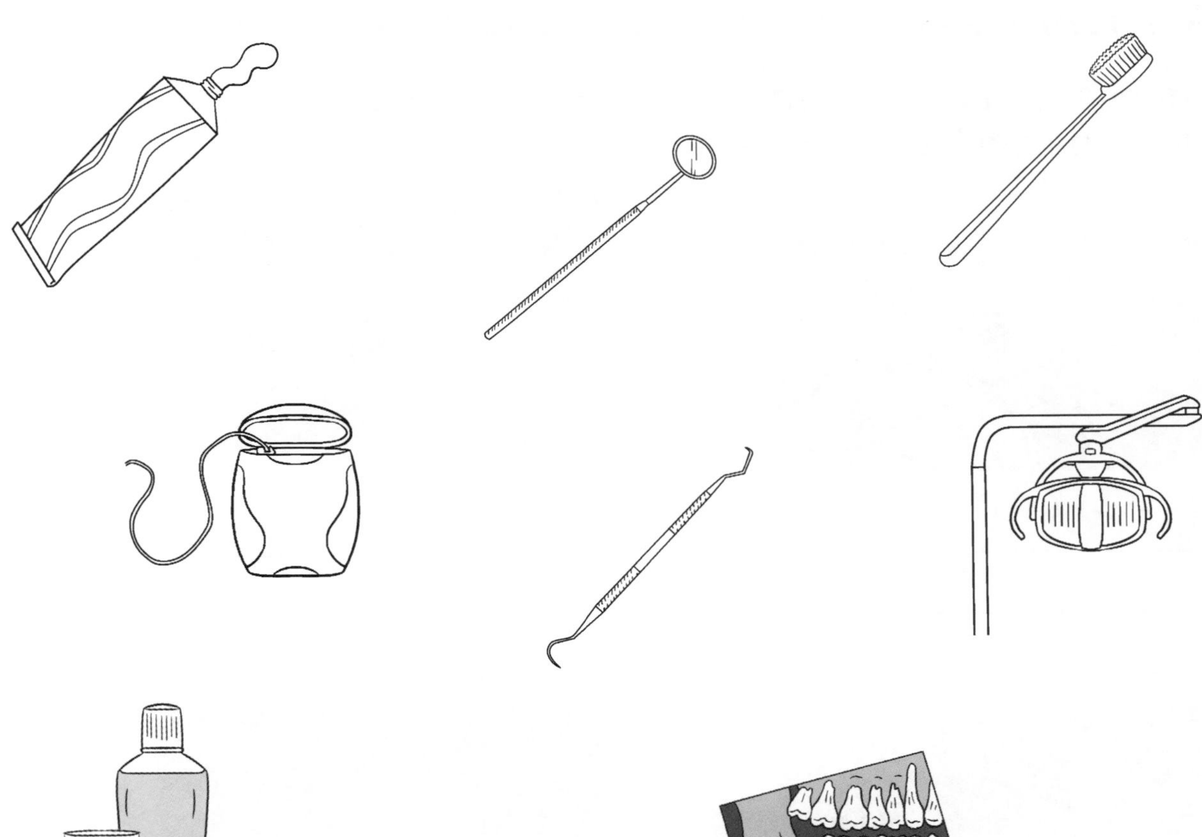

5 Describe how you look after your teeth.

- ____
- ____
- ____
- ____

Date: ____________________

Now look at and think about each of the *I can* statements.

1 Underline the correct word.

A **natural** / **built** environment has been changed by humans.

2 Label each environment either **natural** or **built**.
Describe each environment.

3 Draw lines to match the most suitable habitat to each animal. Explain why you chose that habitat.

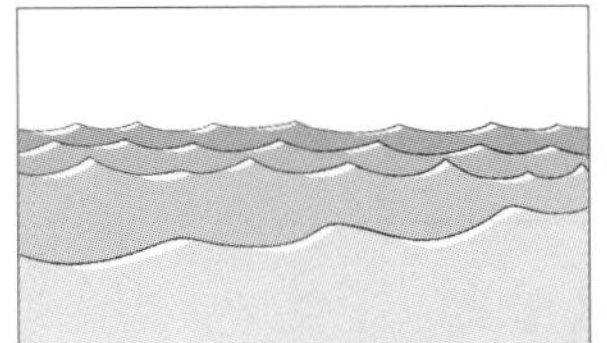 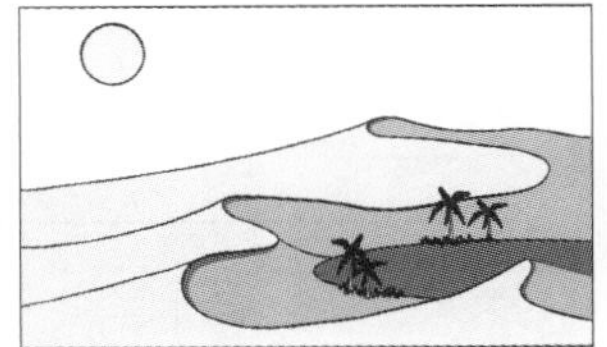  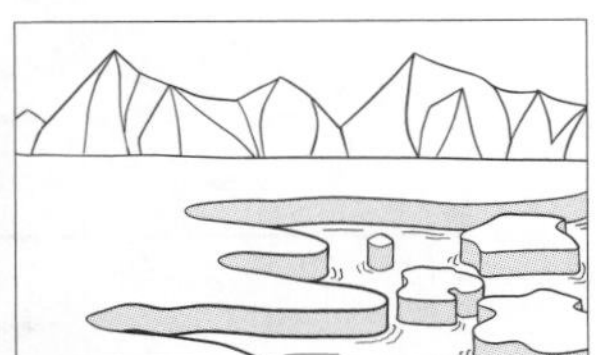

a I chose this habitat for the ____________________

because ____.

b I chose this habitat for the ____________________

because ____.

c I chose this habitat for the ____________________

because ____.

d I chose this habitat for the ____________________

because ____.

4 Choose a word from the box that describes the body covering for each animal.

shell	feathers	hair

5 Name the skin covering and body parts that are the same for a polar bear and a human.

____

____

6 Look at the picture. Which features are the same for a baby squirrel and an adult squirrel?

____

____

____

7 Look at the picture.

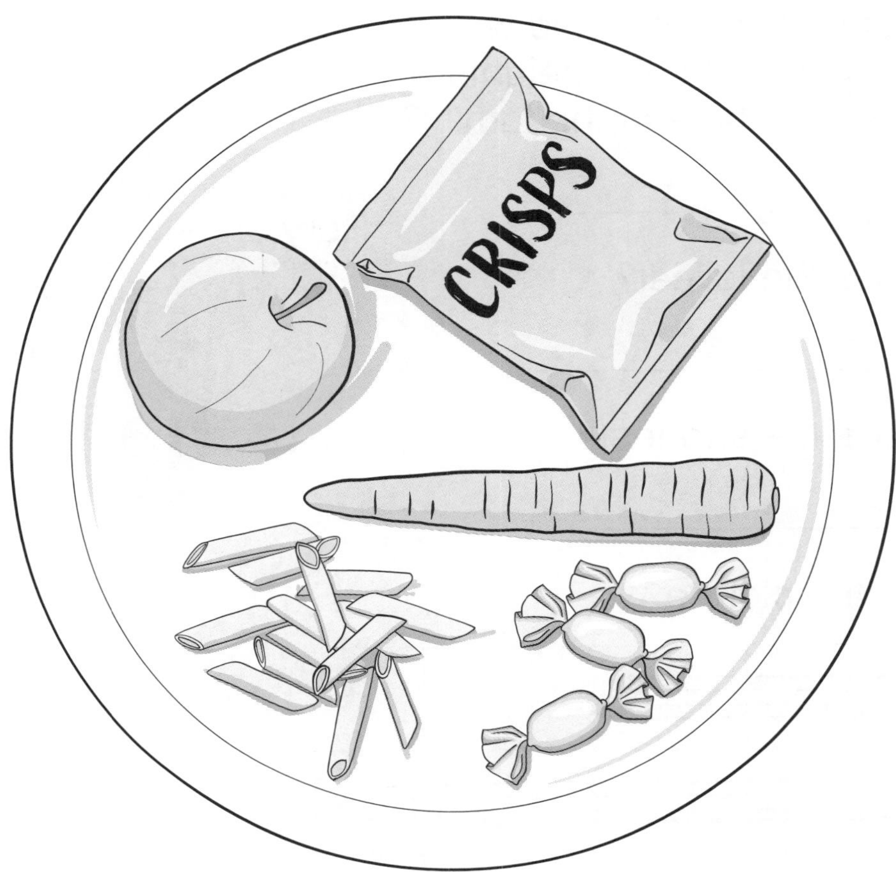

a Cross through the food on the plate that you should not eat too much of.

b Give one more example of a healthy food you should eat more of.

____

8 Which teeth do you use to chew an apple before swallowing it?

____

9 Name three signs of illness you might have if you were sick.

____

Date: ____________________

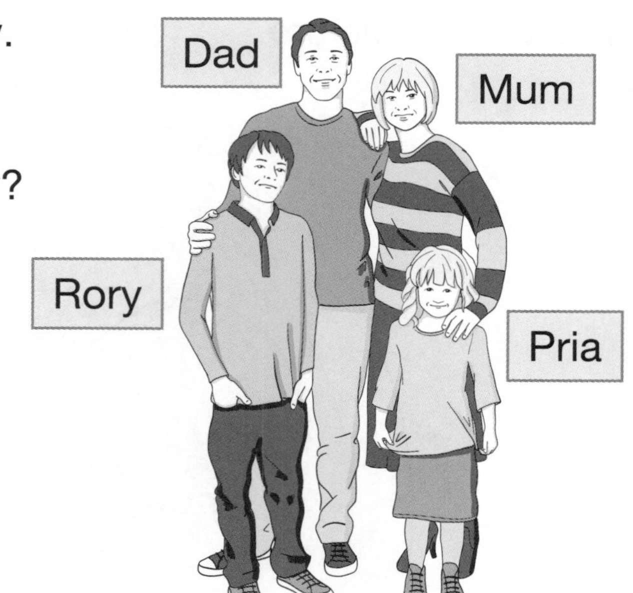

1 Look at the picture of the family.

a What equipment would we use to measure the heights of the members of the family?

b Who is the tallest?

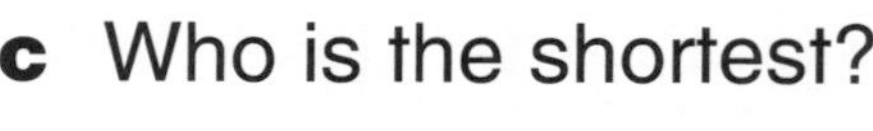

c Who is the shortest?

____

2 Look at the picture.

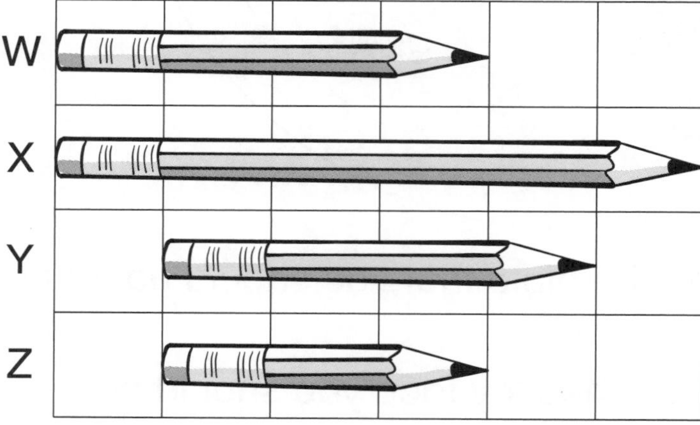

a What is the best way to measure the length of the pencils?

____

b Which pencil is the longest? _______________

c Which pencil is the shortest? _______________

d Which pencils are the same length? _______________

3 Look at the pictures.

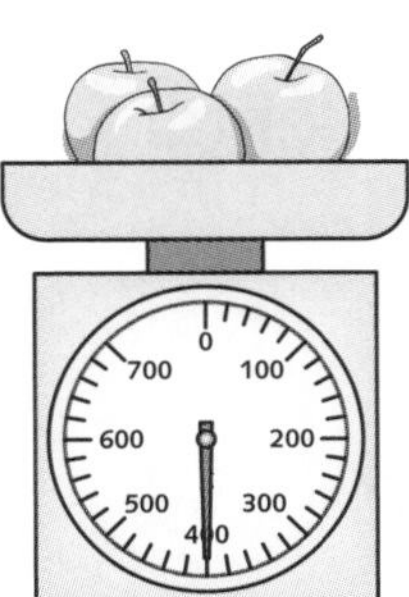
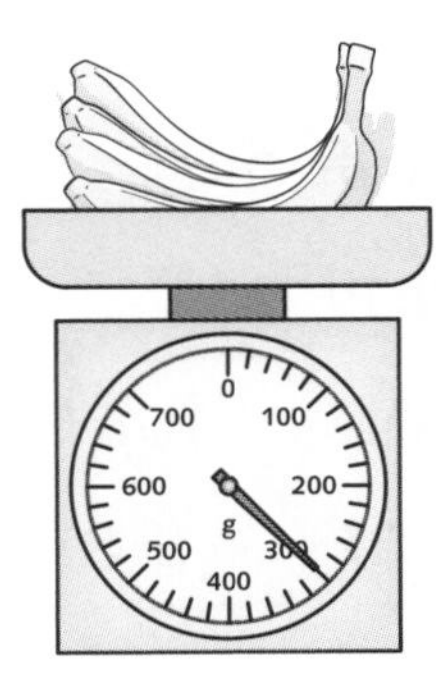
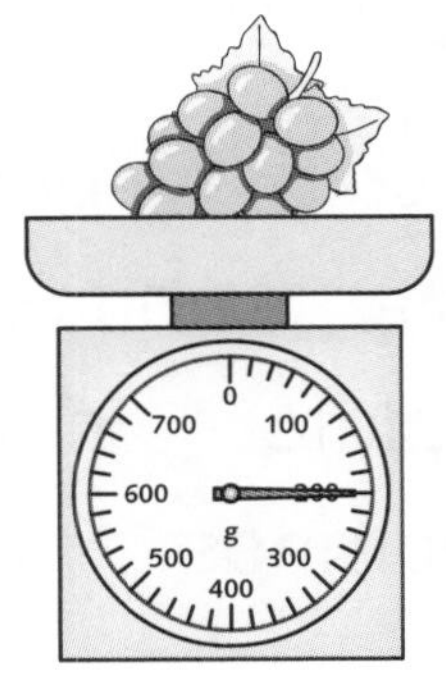
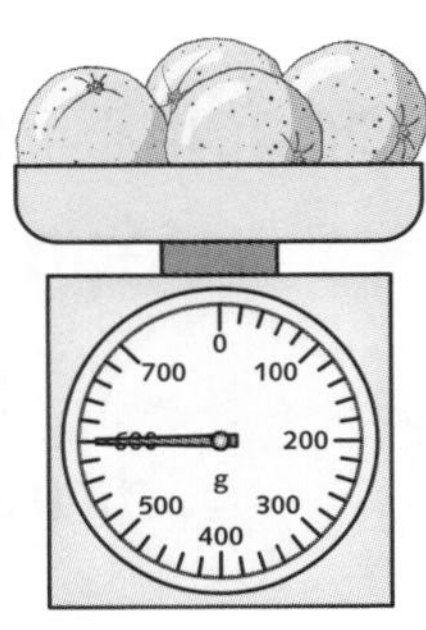

a Circle the correct word in the sentence.

The weighing scales are measuring how **thin** / **heavy** the fruit is.

b Which fruit is the heaviest? ____________________

c Which fruit is the lightest? ____________________

4 Look at the pictures. Write **H** next to the object that you predict will be the heaviest when weighed. Write **L** next to the object that you predict will be the lightest when weighed.

a

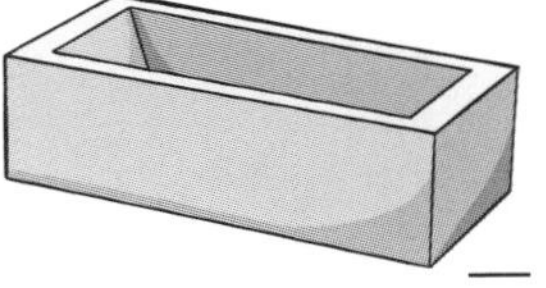 __  __ 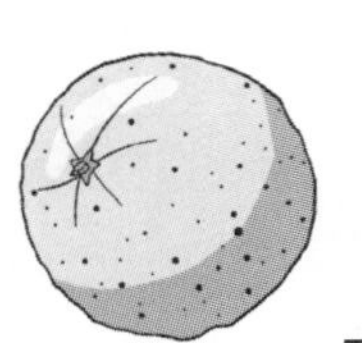 __

b

__  __ 

__

c

__  __  __

d

 __  __  __

Now look at and think about each of the *I can* statements.

Date: ____________________

1 Look at the words in the box. Choose which type of natural material each item is made from. Write the items in the correct columns.

pencil cotton shirt leather briefcase wooden chair
feather duster bricks clay pot silk scarf
paper plate newspaper fur boots
diamond earrings straw hat stone bridge

Plant	Animal	Rock

2 Draw a line to match each natural material to the product made from the material.

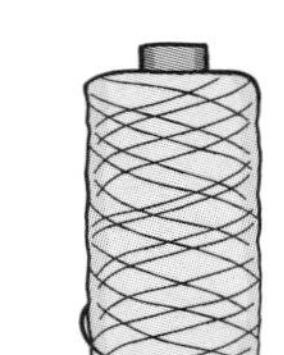

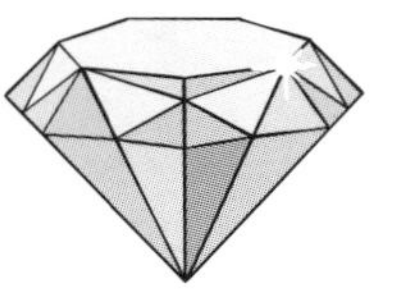

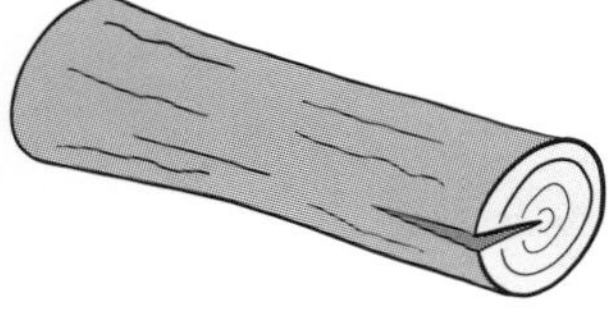

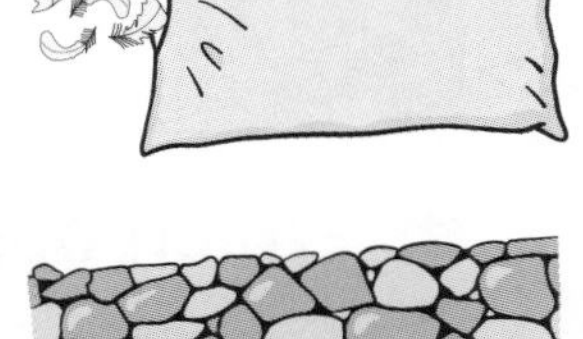

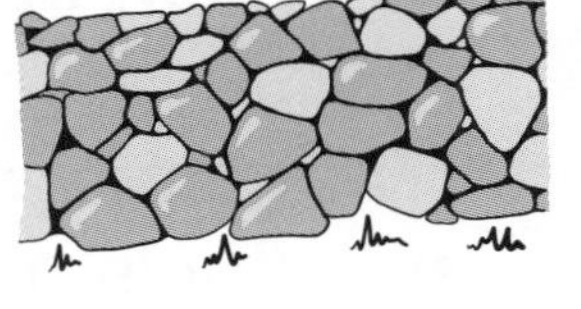

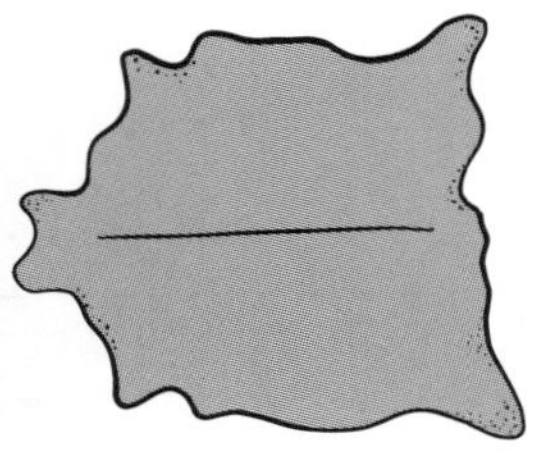

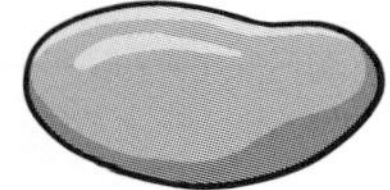

Now look at and think about each of the *I can* statements.

Date: ______________________

1 Look at the pictures.

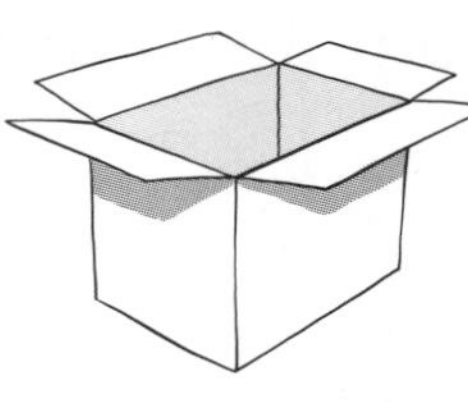

plastic bottle | window | cardboard box

metal fork | umbrella | wooden spoon

a Which objects are waterproof?

____

b Which objects are transparent?

____

c Which objects are smooth?

____

d Why is glass a good material for windows?

____

e Why is metal not a good material for an umbrella?

____

f Which objects are rigid?

____

g Which objects are weak?

____

h Which object is the heaviest?

____

2 a Compare a wooden spoon and a metal spoon.

Property	wooden spoon	metal spoon
Is it hard?		
Is it rough?		
Is it strong?		
Is it flexible?		
Is it light?		
Is it absorbent?		
Is it transparent?		

b How are the wooden spoon and the metal spoon similar?

____

____

c How are the wooden spoon and the metal spoon different?

____

____

Date: ____________________

Now look at and think about each of the *I can* statements.

1 Look at the pictures. Are the objects hard or soft? Write **hard** or **soft** next to each object.

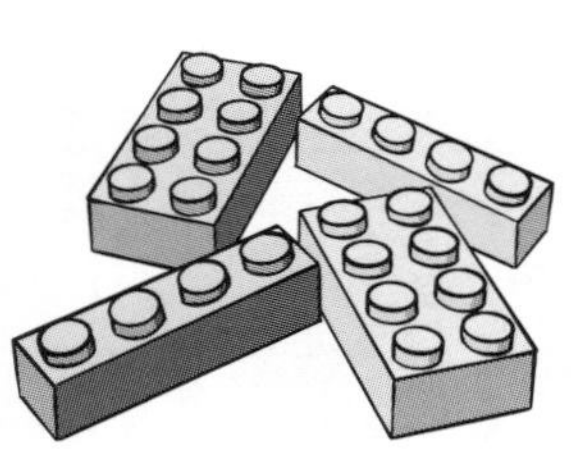

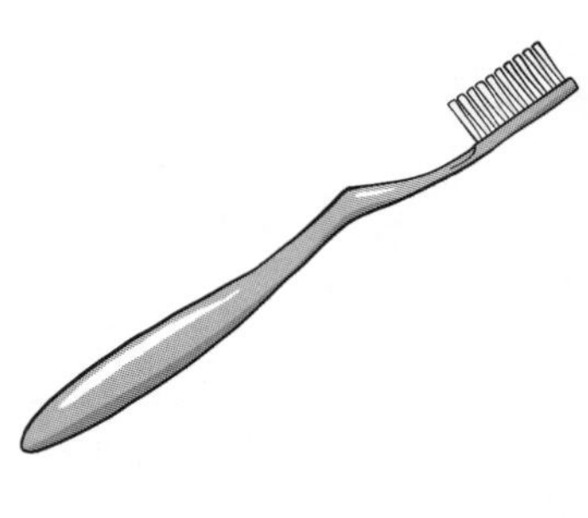

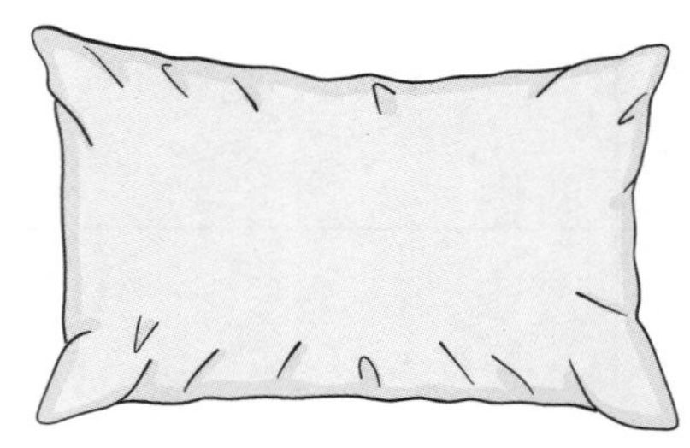

2 Name two different tests you could use to find out whether objects are hard or soft. Describe how to do each test.

3 Look at the pictures of some different materials.

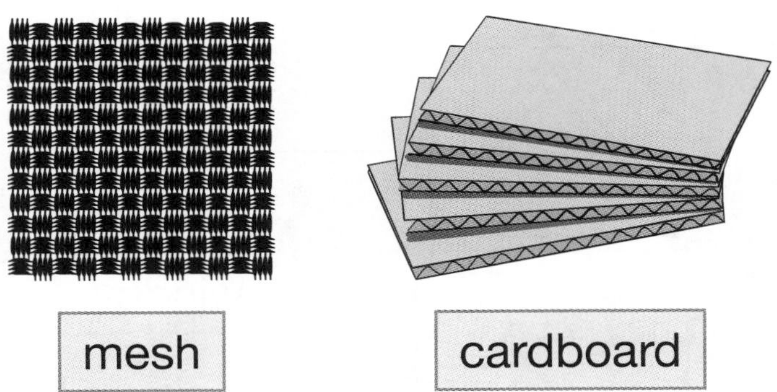

mesh

cardboard

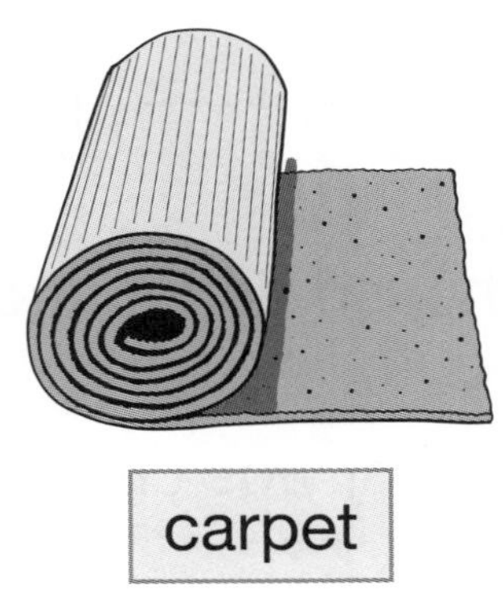

carpet

a Which material is best suited for making a trampoline?

____

b What are the properties of your chosen material?

____

c Why are the other two materials not suitable for a trampoline?

____

____

d Circle the two important properties of a trampoline.

hard rough strong flexible light absorbent transparent

Date: _______________

Now look at and think about each of the *I can* statements.

1 Look at the picture of a house.

a Write an important property of each house part in the third column below.

b Give a reason why you think this material was chosen in the fourth column.

House part	Material	Property	Reason
chimney	bricks		
roof	tiles		
window frame	metal		
window	glass		
door	wood		
walls of house	wood		
front step	bricks		
path	concrete slabs		

2 Choose the best material from the list in the second column to make each object. Give a reason for your choice.

Object	Material options	Reason for choice
umbrella	nylon, clay, cardboard	
water bottle	cardboard, plastic, clay	
duvet cover	clay, metal, cotton	
bicycle	cotton, metal, cardboard	
curtains	fabric, plastic, clay	
balloon	rubber, metal, clay	
bookshelf	nylon, polyester, wood	
pyjamas	metal, cardboard, cotton	
paddling pool	cardboard, plastic, cotton	

Date: ______________________

Now look at and think about each of the *I can* statements.

1 Look at the chart.

a Underline the materials in the first column that have changed chemically.

b Describe how the material was changed.

Material	New material	What happened to change the material?
burning wood	ash/coal	
plate	broken plate	
banana	peeled banana	
egg	fried egg	
pear	rotten pear	
nail	rusted nail	
bread	sliced bread	
cake ingredients	baked cake	

2 Describe how you can change these three materials into different materials.

Material	**What can you do to change the material?**	**Draw a picture to show the new material**
apple		
firework		
yellow and red pots of paint red paint yellow paint		

Now look at and think about each of the *I can* statements.

Date: ______________________

1 Look at the chart. Compare the two surfboards.

	Old style surfboard	New style surfboard
		splash
How is the shape different?		
What does the new style surfboard have that is not on the old style surfboard?		
What materials are used for each surfboard?		
How has the change in material used improved the new style surfboard?		

2 **a** Look at the chart. Compare the two running shoes.

	Old style running shoe	**New style running shoe**
How is the shape different?		
What materials are used for each running shoe?		
How has the change in material used improved the new style running shoes?		

b The new style running shoe is lighter than the old running shoe. Explain why you think this is important.

____

____

____

____

Now look at and think about each of the *I can* statements.

Date: ____________________

1 Look at each picture. Is the force a push or pull? Write **push** or **pull** under the picture.

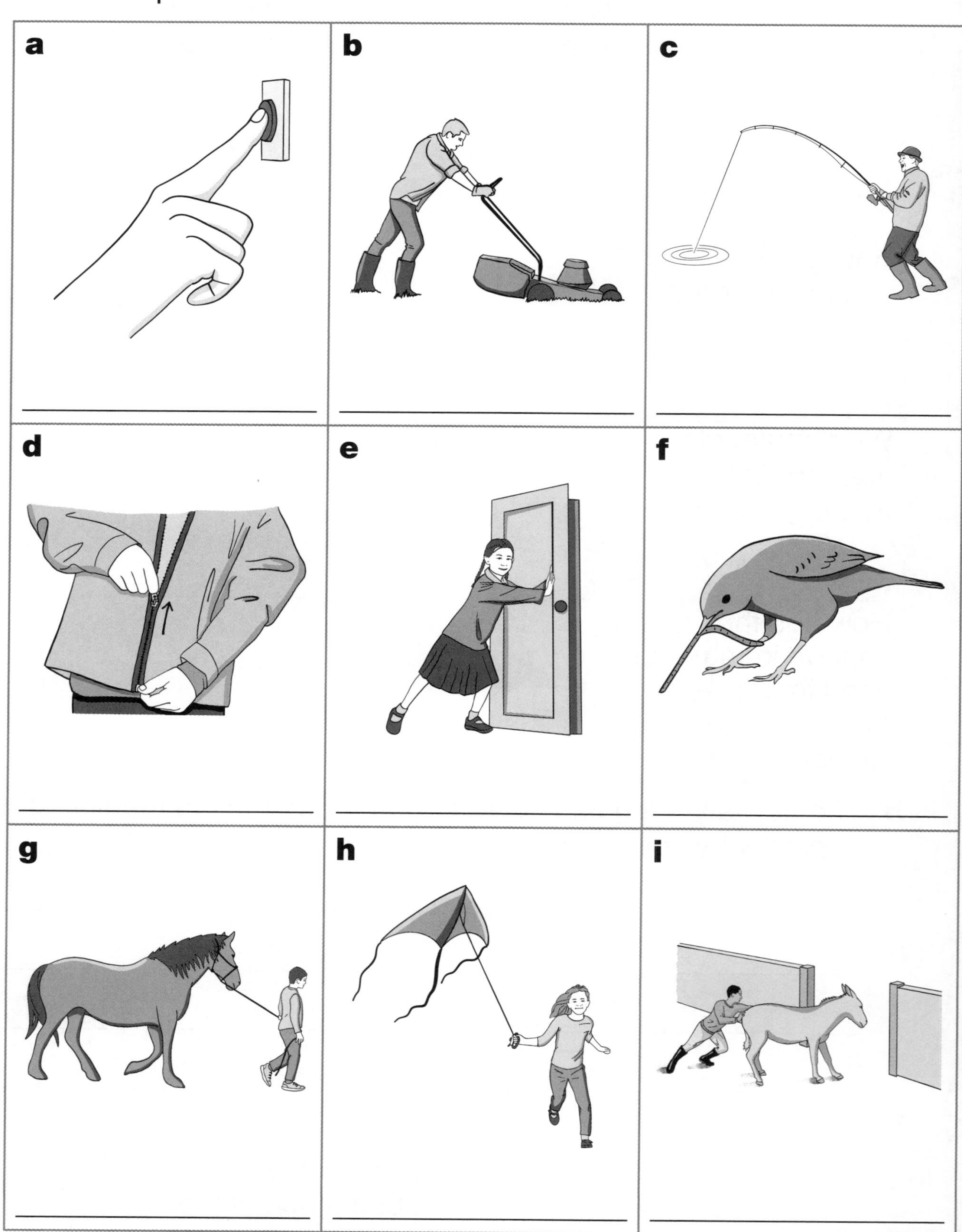

2 Look at the picture of the boy playing with a yo-yo.

a Add push and pull arrows to the picture.

b Describe how pushing and pulling forces make the yo-yo move.

____

____

____

____

Date: ____________________

Now look at and think about each of the *I can* statements.

1 Look at each picture. Is it better to push or pull the object? Circle your answer.

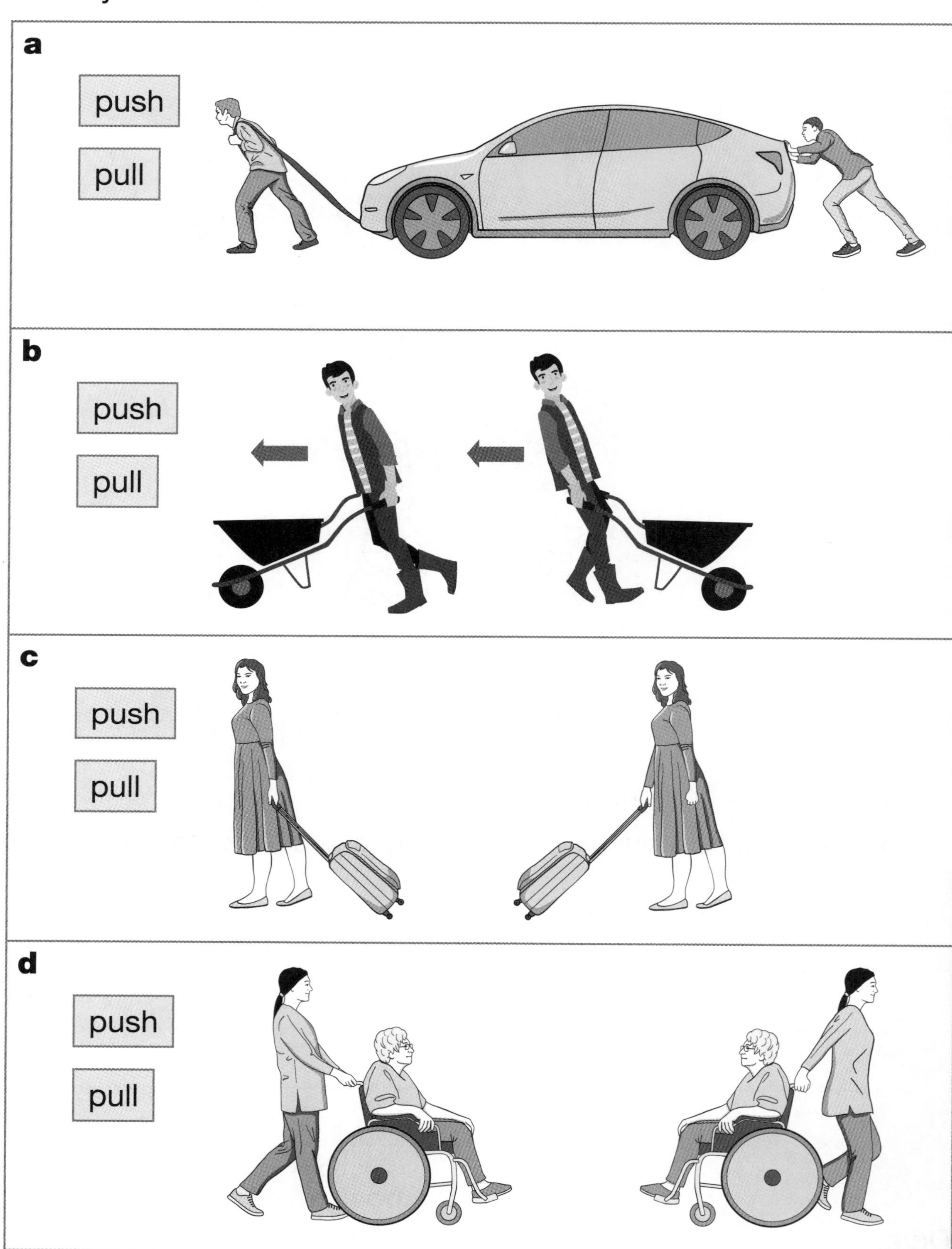

2 Descibe how a person can stop the movement of each object.

a	______________________ ______________________ ______________________ ______________________
b	______________________ ______________________ ______________________ ______________________
c	______________________ ______________________ ______________________ ______________________
d	______________________ ______________________ ______________________ ______________________

Date: ______________________

Now look at and think about each of the *I can* statements.

1 Look at the pictures of clay. What type of force is being used to change the shape of the clay? Circle the correct word for each picture.

Clay	Force word
	squash squeeze stretch bend twist
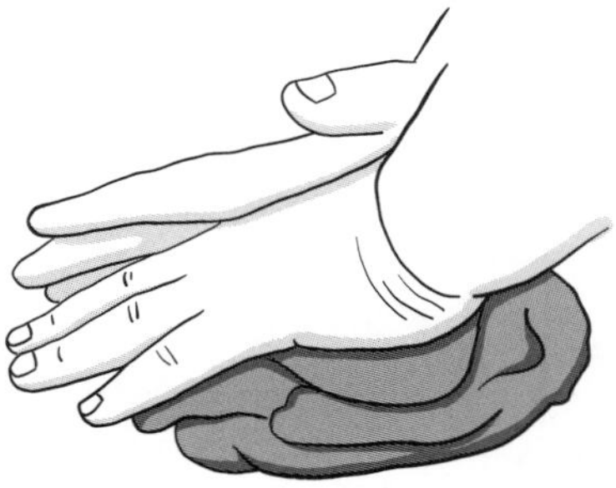	squash squeeze stretch bend twist
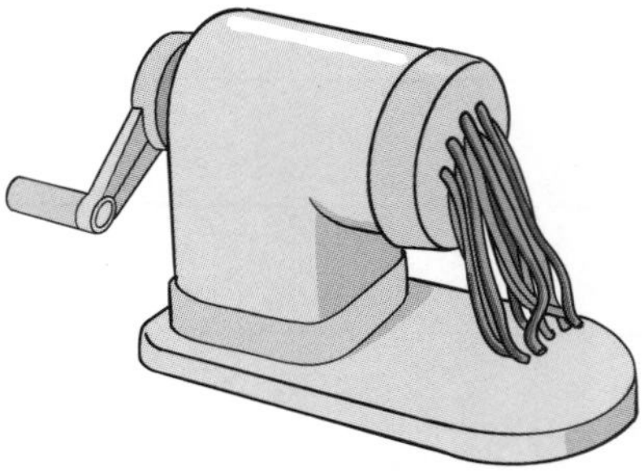	squash squeeze stretch bend twist
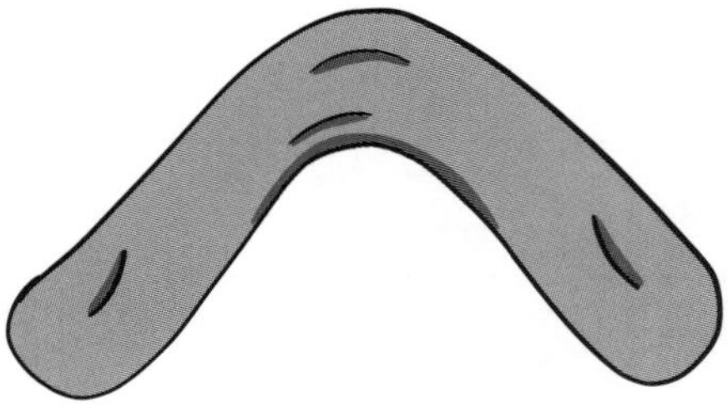	squash squeeze stretch bend twist
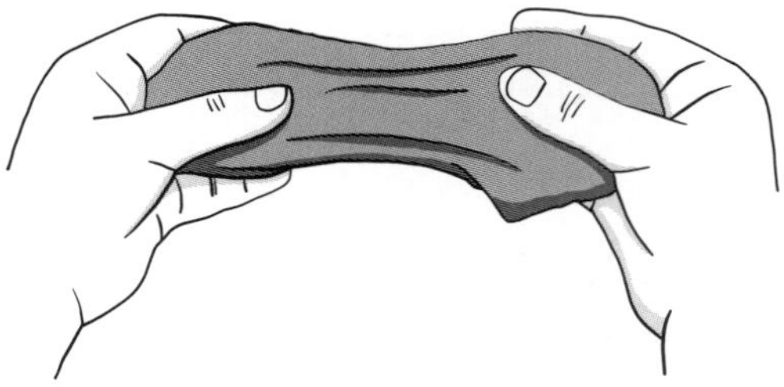	squash squeeze stretch bend twist

2 Look at the pictures.

a		Has the force on the car helped or damaged it? ______________________
b	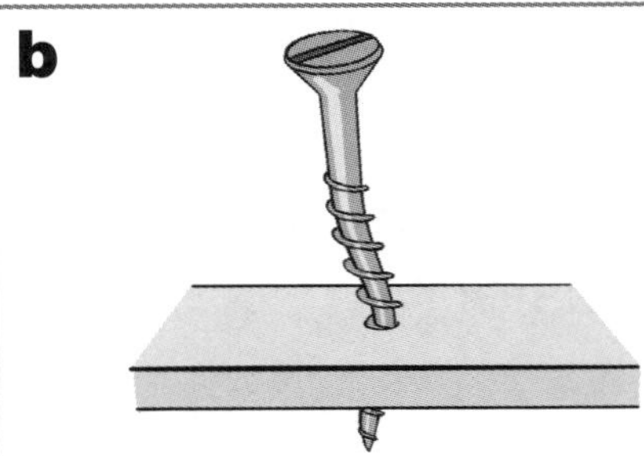	Has the force on the screw helped or damaged it? ______________________
c	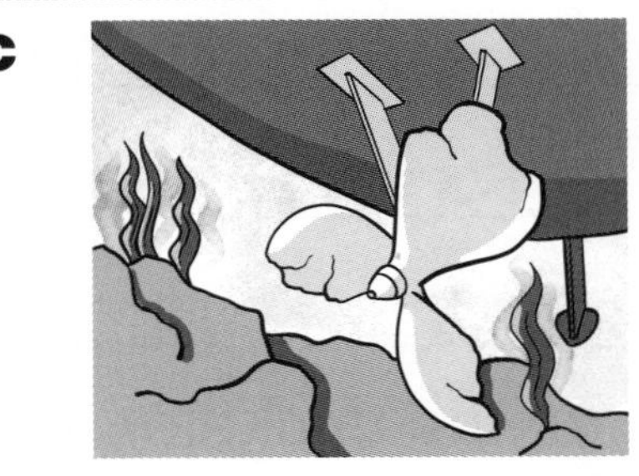	Has the force on the propeller helped or damaged it? ______________________

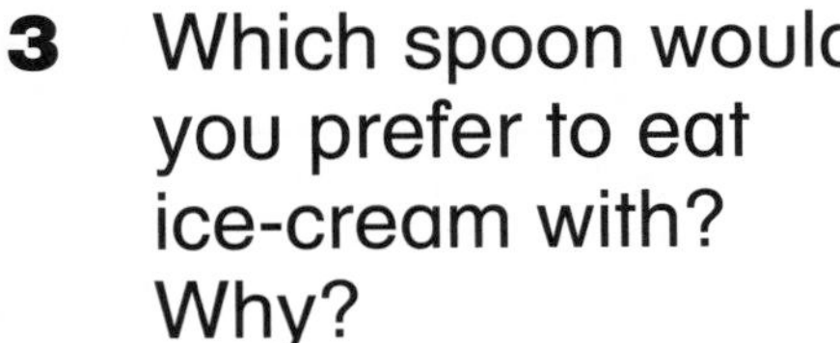

3 Which spoon would you prefer to eat ice-cream with? Why?

____

____

____

____

Date: ______________________

Now look at and think about each of the *I can* statements.

1 Look at the pictures. Then answer the questions.

a How can the boy make the bicycle move more slowly?

____

____

____

____

b How can the girl make the ball move faster?

____

____

____

____

c How can the cricketer make the ball move faster?

____

____

____

____

d How can the skier make her skis move faster?

____

____

____

____

2 Three identical erasers are dropped from the same height at the same time.

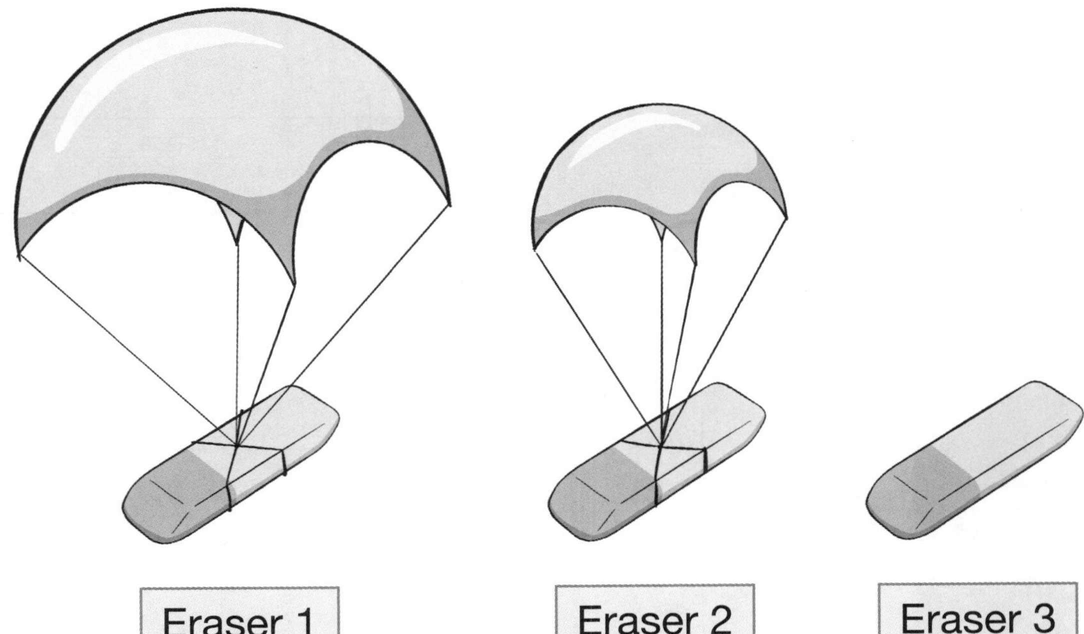

a Which eraser will hit the ground first?

____

b Which eraser will hit the ground second?

____

c Which eraser will hit the ground third?

____

d Why will the erasers land on the ground at different times?

____

Now look at and think about each of the *I can* statements.

Date: _______________

1 Describe how the direction of movement can be changed in these pictures.

a

b

c

d

e

2 Look at the picture. Then answer the questions.

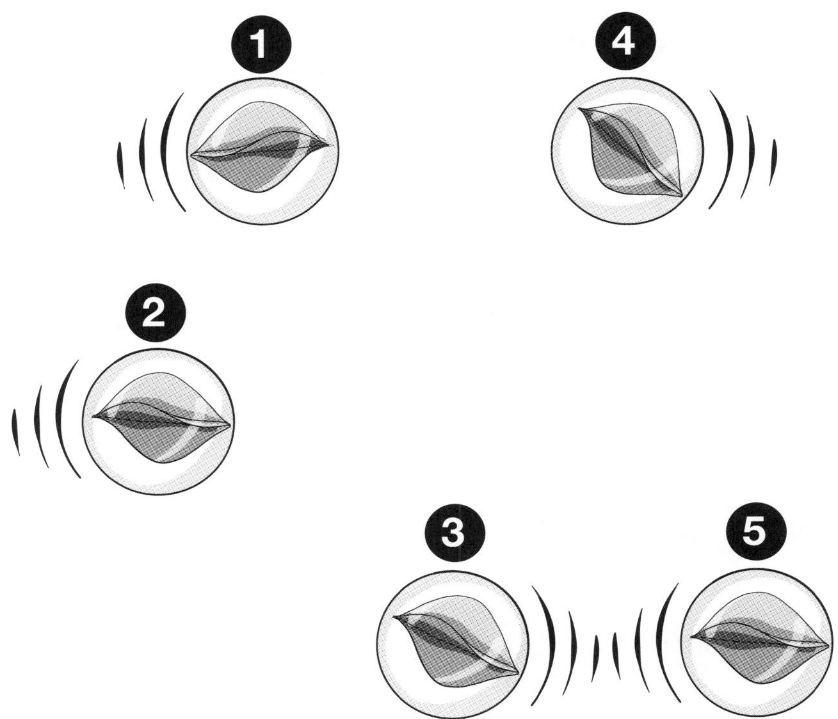

a Draw an arrow above each marble to show the direction it is moving in.

b What happened to marbles 3 and 5? Has this made the marbles move faster or slower?

____

____

c What do you think will happen to marbles 1 and 4?

____

d What will happen to marble 2? Explain why you think this.

____

____

Date: ____________________

Now look at and think about each of the *I can* statements.

1 Complete the chart by drawing pictures of the missing information in the boxes.

Natural material	Manufactured material

2 Tick (✓) the boxes that describe the properties of the materials.

	wooden table	paper plate	glass bottle	metal key	plastic cup	cotton shirt
hard						
soft						
smooth						
rough						
waterproof						
absorbent						
strong						
fragile						

3 Draw a picture of a chemical change to each material.

Material	Chemical change
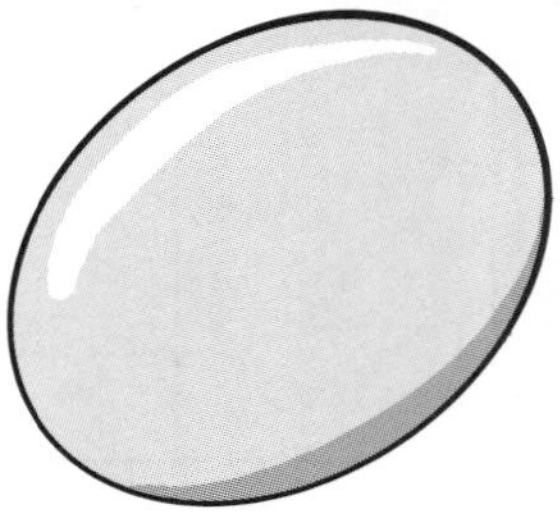	

4 Draw a picture of a push or a pull in each box.

Push	Pull

5 Draw an arrow on each picture to show the direction the ball is moving in.

a

How can the ball move faster?

____

How can the ball slow down?

____

How can the ball change direction?

____

b

How can the ball move faster?

____

How can the ball slow down?

____

How can the ball change direction?

____

c

How can the ball move faster?

____

How can the ball slow down?

____

How can the ball change direction?

____

Date: ______________________

1 Look at the pictures. Tick (✓) the sources of light.

2 **a** Circle all the useful light sources in this picture.

b Are the lights in the picture natural or human-made?

____

c How is each light in the picture useful?

____

____

____

d Which lights still need to work during the day?

____

3 Look at the picture of the forest scene during the day.

a Draw what you will see in the forest as the Sun sets over the hill.

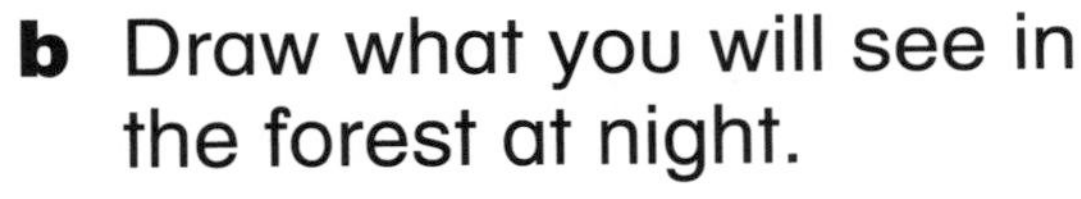

b Draw what you will see in the forest at night.

c Draw what you will see in the forest at night if you have a torch.

Now look at and think about each of the *I can* statements.

Date: ______________________

1 a Tick the sources of light that we mainly use in our homes now.

b Circle the light sources that do not use electricity.

2 Look at the picture. Circle the light sources in the house.

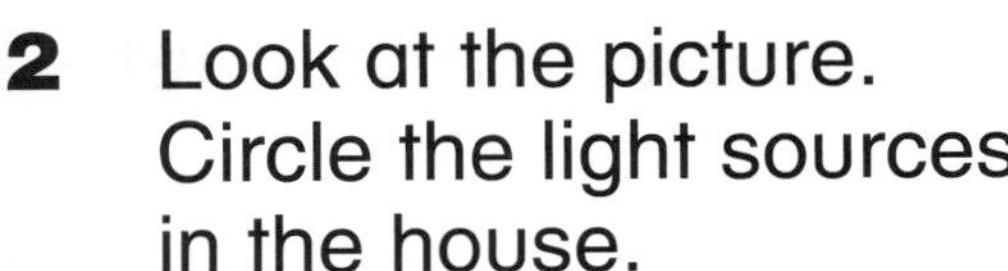

3 Tick (✓) the rooms where the following light sources are found.

Light source	bathroom	kitchen	dining room	lounge	bedroom	study
fluorescent tube						
long-life lamp (compact fluorescent)						
filament lamp						
halogen lamp						
LED						
computer screen						
TV screen						

Date: ______________________

Now look at and think about each of the *I can* statements.

1 Label each picture to show the Sun's position at **sunrise**, **sunset** and **midday**.

2 Complete the sentence.

The shadow on the picture tells us that it is ____________________.

3 The Sun is rising in the picture.
Draw a picture in the box showing the Sun setting.

4 Complete the sentences. Use the words in the box.

Earth east sky west

The Sun rises in the ________________.

The Sun sets in the ________________.

The Sun appears to move across the ________________ during the day, but it is actually the ________________ that is moving.

Now look at and think about each of the *I can* statements.

Date: ________________

1 Tick (✓) the kitchen appliances that need electricity to work.

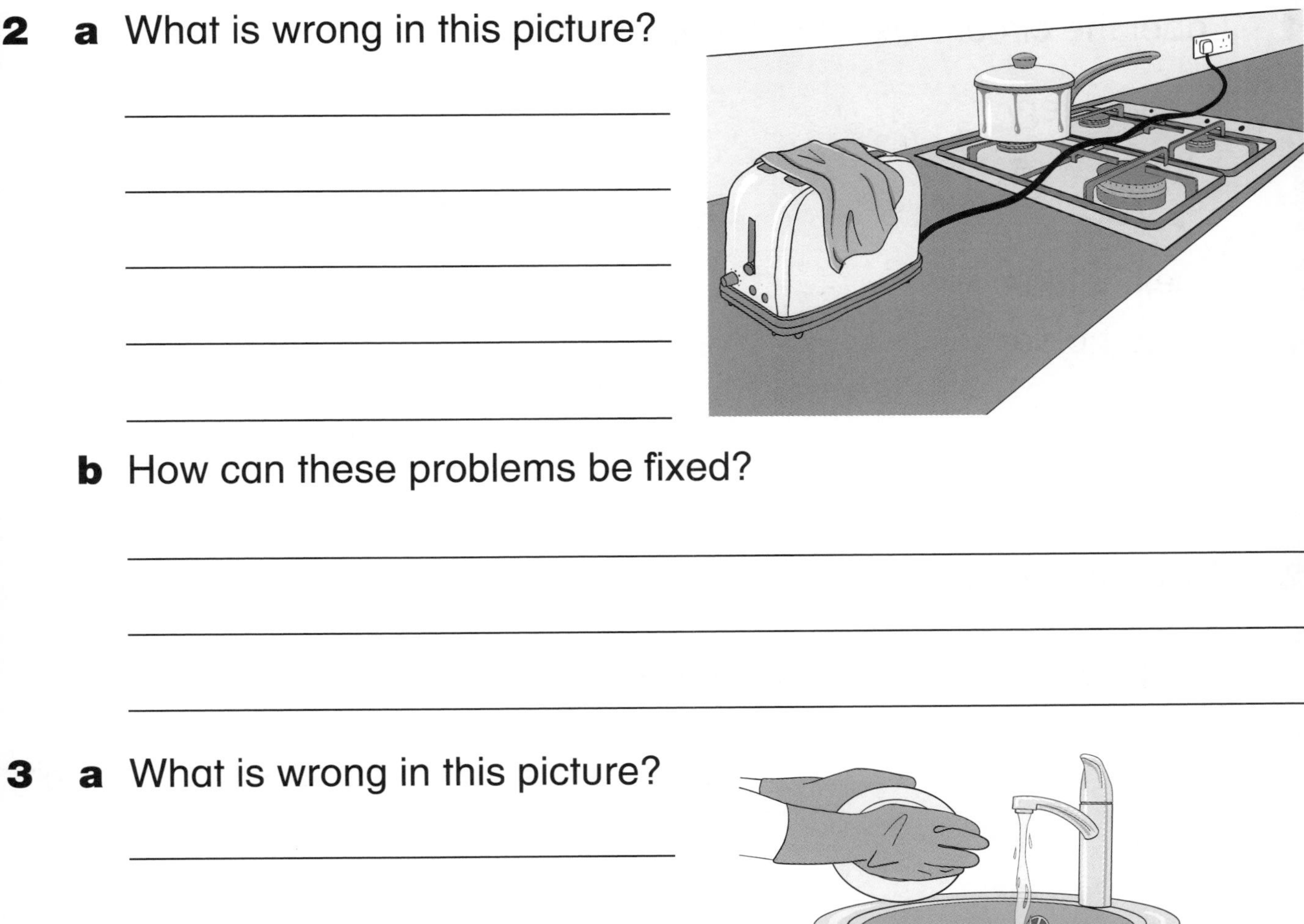

2 **a** What is wrong in this picture?

b How can these problems be fixed?

3 **a** What is wrong in this picture?

b How can these problems be fixed?

Date: ______________________

Now look at and think about each of the *I can* statements.

1 Label the circuit. Use the words in the box.

cell/battery
metal wire
lamp
cell holder
lamp holder

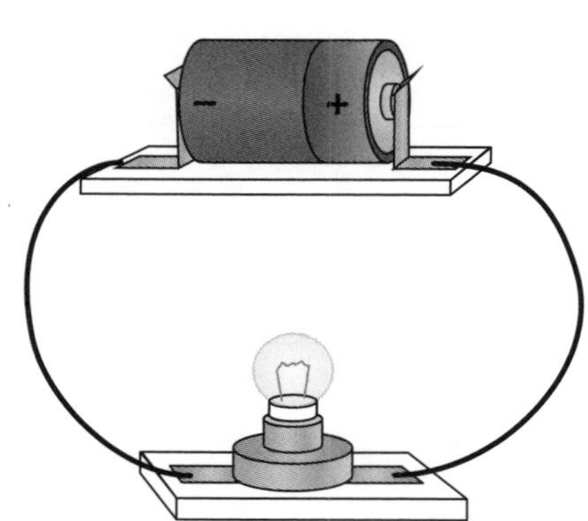

2 Draw lines to match each component to its picture and function.

Picture	Component	Function
	cell	stores the electricity
+	cell holder	connects the parts of the circuit
	lamp	lights up
	wire	holds the lamp in place
	lamp holder	holds the cell in place

3 Use the components to draw a closed circuit.

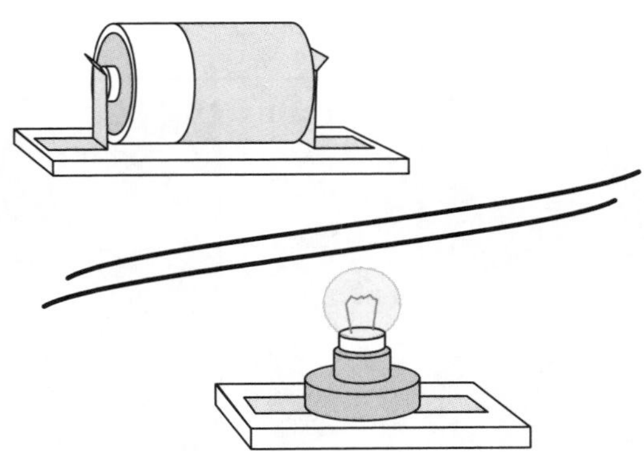

4 Why will the lamp not light up in these circuits?

Circuit	Reason the lamp will not light up
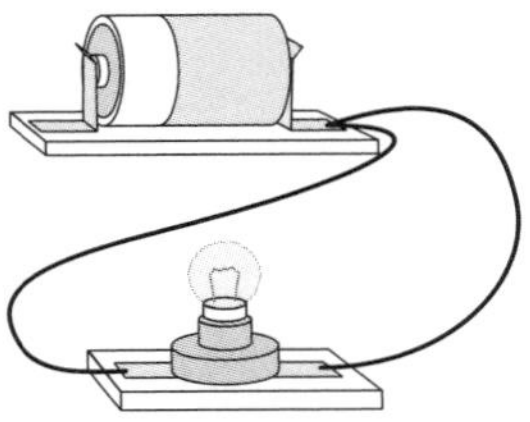	
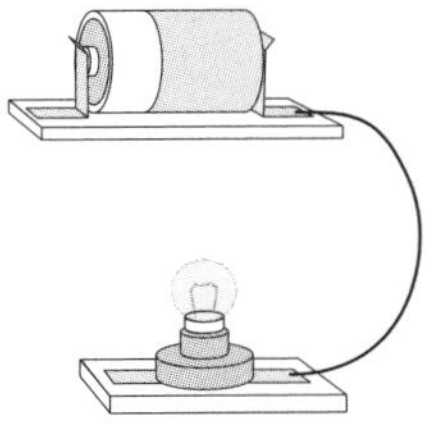	
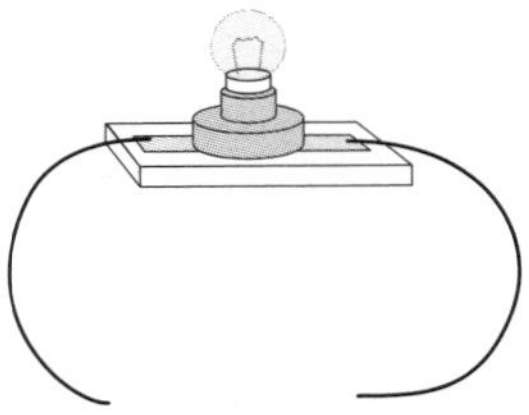	
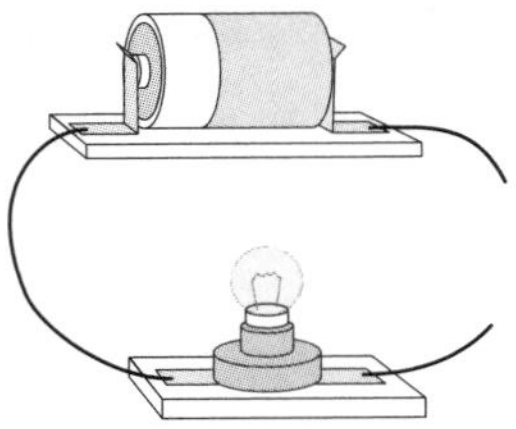	

Date: ______________________________

Now look at and think about each of the *I can* statements.

1 Look at the pictures. Describe how mining has changed the natural environment.

2 Use the words in the box to complete the sentences.

coal	holes	mountains	habitats	pollute
jobs	crust	tunnels	minerals	Earth

a People mine materials out of the Earth's ______________________.

b The materials mined from the Earth are stone,

______________________, oil and ______________________.

c Some mines are underground, with long, deep

______________________.

d Some mines are on the surface of the Earth and are wide, open

______________________.

e Mines change the Earth's surface and change the forests,

______________________, deserts and seas where they are taking

materials from the ______________________.

f Animal and plant ______________________ are destroyed where the mines are built.

g Mining can also ______________________ the air, water and land, which kills everything that lives there.

h Mining does create ______________________ for people.

Date: ______________________

Now look at and think about each of the *I can* statements.

1 Draw lines to match the pictures of different rocks to their names. Circle whether they are hard or soft rocks.

Rock	Name of rock
 	granite (hard / soft)
 	limestone (hard / soft)
	sandstone (hard / soft)
	slate (hard / soft)
	marble (hard / soft)

2 Draw lines to match each rock to its use.

Slate: It is a strong rock that is good for tiling. It is waterproof and smooth.

Sandstone: It is strong and can last a long time. It is used for building, statues and fountains.

Granite: It is a waterproof rock that comes in many different colours. It can be cut, carved and shaped for building.

Marble: It is a fireproof rock but it is not waterproof. It is used for walls, floors, steps and columns by builders.

Diamonds: They are hard rocks that cannot be scratched or damaged. Most of these rocks are transparent.

Limestone: It is an absorbent, soft rock. It is often made into a powder that is used to make glass or as cement.

Now look at and think about each of the *I can* statements.

Date: ______________________

1 Look at the pictures showing the different types of mining.

a 

This mining is known as

______________________.

How does this mining work? ______________

____

____

____

____

b 

This mining is known as

______________________.

How does this mining work? ______________

____

____

____

____

c

This mining is known as

______________________.

How does this mining work? ______________

____

____

____

____

2 Use the words in the box to complete the sentences about mining in Madagascar.

sapphires	forests	rivers	gold	environment	mining

a Madagascar is well-known for its ____________________, animals and minerals.

b It is a poor country, where most of the people earn a living by

____________________.

c They mine ____________________ and sapphires, using their own simple equipment.

d The miners damage the natural ____________________ where they mine.

e They make deep pits to find ____________________.

f They look in ____________________ to find gold.

3 How can the people in Madagascar help to fix the damage from mining?

____

____

____

____

____

____

Date: ____________________

Now look at and think about each of the *I can* statements.

1 Is each object a light source? If it is a light source, is it natural or human-made? Complete the table.

Object	Light source	Natural or human-made light source?
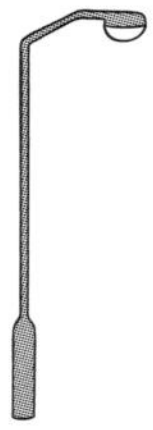	Yes / No	
	Yes / No	
	Yes / No	
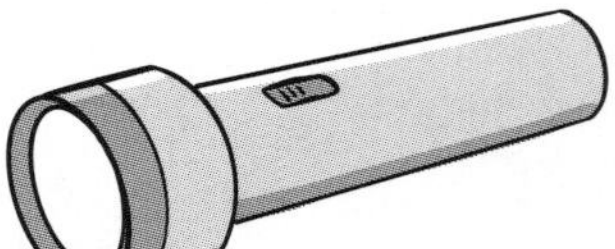	Yes / No	
	Yes / No	
	Yes / No	

2 Create a closed electric circuit with the following materials.

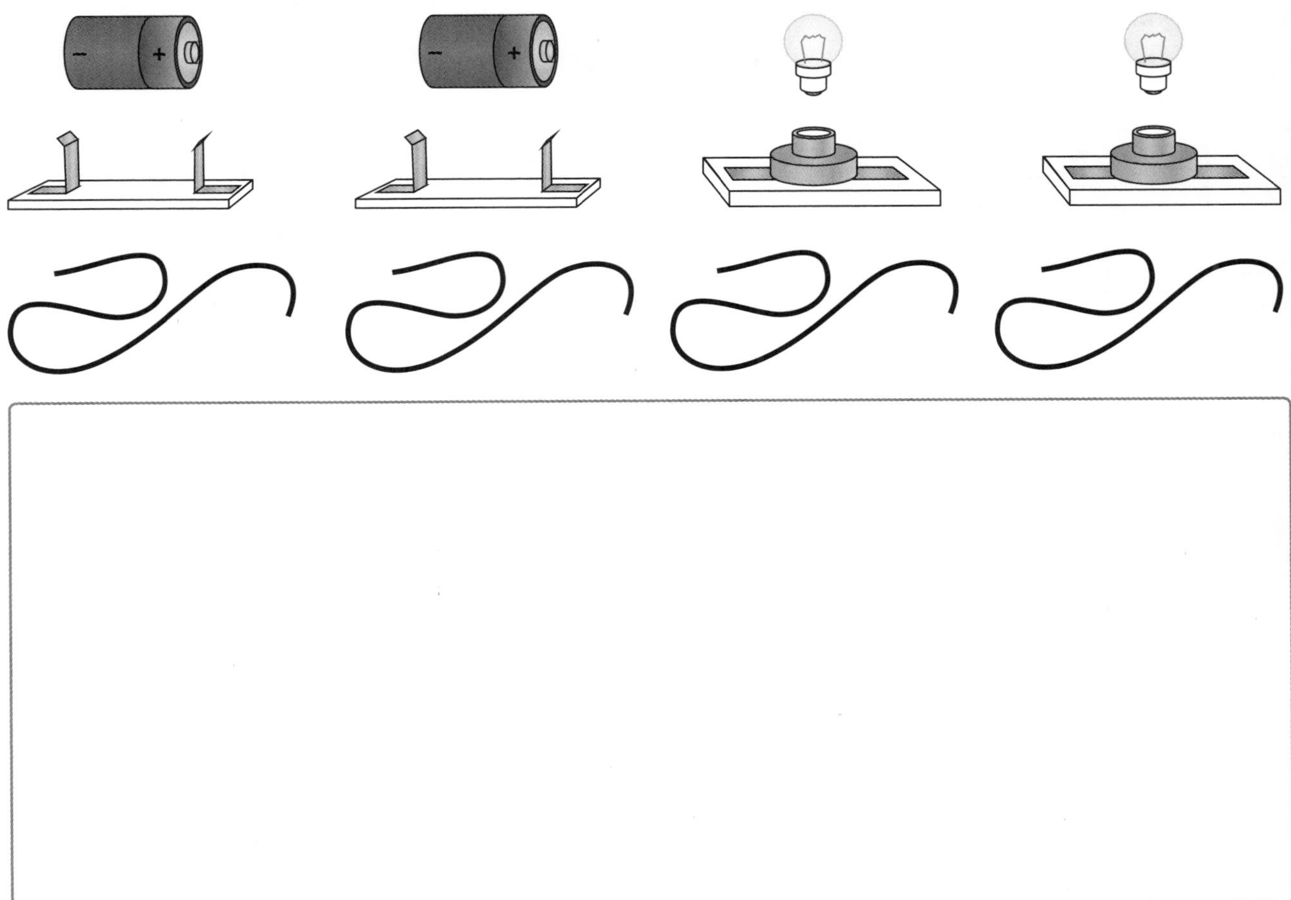

3 What is wrong with each of these electric circuits?

	____________________ ____________________ ____________________
	____________________ ____________________ ____________________
	____________________ ____________________ ____________________

4 Draw lines to match each stone to its properties and to its uses.

Properties	Stone	Uses
It is an absorbent, soft rock.	limestone	It is a strong rock that is good for tiling.
It is strong and can last a long time.	slate	It is often made into a powder that is used to make glass or cement.
It is a waterproof rock that comes in different colours.	sandstone	It is used for walls, floors, steps and columns.
It is waterproof and smooth.	marble	It is used for building, statues and fountains.
It is a fireproof rock but it is not waterproof.	granite	It can be cut, carved and shaped for building.

5 Draw linking lines to match the mining pictures to their descriptions.

Underground mines are tunnels deep in the Earth's crust. Minerals are dug out of these mines.

Some minerals are dug out of the ground in riverbeds.

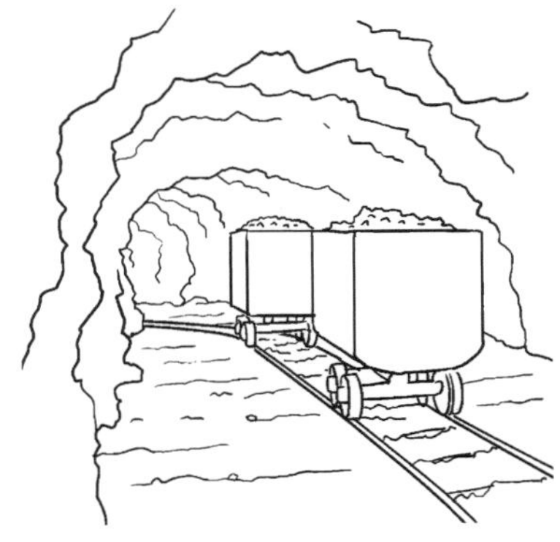

Open-pit mines are big, deep open holes in the ground. Minerals and stone are dug out of these mines.

6 How is mining harmful?

____

7 How is mining useful?

____

Date: ____________________

Acknowledgements

Photo acknowledgements

The publishers gratefully acknowledge the permission granted to reproduce the copyright material in this book. Every effort has been made to trace copyright holders and to obtain their permission for the use of copyright material. The publishers will gladly receive any information enabling them to rectify any error or omission at the first opportunity.

P16tl Gballgiggsphoto/Shutterstock; p16tr SeventyFour/Shutterstock; p16bl New Africa/Shutterstock; p16br PeopleImages.com – Yuri A/Shutterstock; p17 Coerie Ferreira/Shutterstock; p18t QQQQQQQT/Shutterstock; p18ct Dashu Xinganling/Shutterstock; p18c Irina Markova/Shutterstock; p18cb Arnain/Shutterstock; p18b Ko Zatu/Shutterstock; p36tl Pisaphotography/Shutterstock; p36tr Vixitc/Shutterstock; p36cl Salvador Aznar/Shutterstock; p36cr David Ball/Alamy Stock Photo; p36b TSN52/Shutterstock; p59t idesygn/Shutterstock; p64tr Kritthima/Shutterstock; p64tl Eric Isselee/Shutterstock; p64cl Muratart/Shutterstock; p64cr Pio3/Shutterstock; p64bl Bjoern Wylezich/Shutterstock; p64br Biskariot/Shutterstock; p74tl Nevodka/Shutterstock; p74tr Graja/Shutterstock; p74ctl Target Shot/Shutterstock; p74ctr HomeArt/Shutterstock; p74cbl Tatiana Popova/Shutterstock; p74cbr ApoGapo/Shutterstock; p74bl ApoGapo/Shutterstock; p74br Lazy_Bear/Shutterstock; p78tl MIGUEL G. SAAVEDRA/Shutterstock; p78tr Nada B/Shutterstock; p78bl Witold Skrypczak/Alamy Stock Photo; p78br Olena Vasylieva/Alamy Stock Photo; p80t Stacy Funderburke/Shutterstock; p80ct Oleksii Sagitov/Shutterstock; p80c Marafona/Shutterstock; p88cb Mg1408/Shutterstock; p88b Kues/Shutterstock; p81t Totsaporn/Shutterstock; p81ctt Gojalicilik/Shutterstock; p81ct T.W. van Urk/Shutterstock; p81cb Sirisak_baokaew/Shutterstock; p81cbb Mark S Johnson/Shutterstock; p81b Nata-Lia/Shutterstock; p83 Homo Cosmicos/Shutterstock.